Stratford, China:
A Long Poem

Martin Avery

ISBN 978-1-312-38058-5
Copyright © Martin Avery, 2014

Introduction: Stratford, China, is a new book made up of two long poems describing one summertime road trip to Stratford, Ontario, Canada, during the summer of 2014, while I was in Toronto, home from China, after a year abroad, which gave me this great idea: China could copy Stratford and re-create it China-style somewhere like the JinShiTan part of Dalian, in Dongbei, or north-east China, where the Black Mountains make a great back-drop for the Yellow Sea and we have the best air in Asia not to mention the best seafood plus a lot of other great food and life is good but the little city of six million could use a major attraction like Stratford to lift it onto the world stage.

Stratford, China
A Long Poem

Martin Avery

"When women love us, they forgive us everything, even our crimes; when they do not love us, they give us credit for nothing, not even our virtues."
Honore de Balzac

"A lover always thinks of his mistress first and himself second; with a husband it runs the other way."
Honore de Balzac

"The more one judges, the less one loves."
Honore de Balzac

"There is no such thing as a great talent without great will power."
Honore de Balzac

"True love is eternal, infinite, and always like itself. It is equal and pure, without violent demonstrations: it is seen with white hairs and is always young in the heart."
Honore de Balzac

Come not between the dragon and his wrath. (1.1.124)
William Shakespeare, King Lear

We two alone will sing like birds i' the cage:
When thou dost ask me blessing, I'll kneel down,
And ask of thee forgiveness: and we'll live,
And pray, and sing, and tell old tales, and laugh
At gilded butterflies, and hear poor rogues
Talk of court news; and we'll talk with them too,
Who loses, and who wins; who's in, who's out;
And take upon 's the mystery of things,
As if we were God's spies; and we'll wear out,
In a walled prison, packs and sets of great ones
That ebb and flow by the moon. (5.3.9)
William Shakespeare, King Lear

There's something bout the bright lights
You find them on the right nights
Forces you just can't fight
You're trouble but it's alright (yeah)
Take control, please own me
Only love can save me

You're whole lotta crazy
I think you like it too
But let me tell you baby
I'm so crazy for you
So lose your mind, you psycho
I think I like it too
I gotta tell you baby
I'm so crazy for you

So crazy (oh)
So crazy (ooh)
So crazy, baby
I'm so crazy for you

- from "Crazy For You" by Jacob William Hoggard

1. Introducing Balzac And Fellini

BreakFast With Balzac, Lunchtime With Fellini
is a long poem chronicling a summertime
road trip to Stratford, Ontario, for the
Shakespeare Festival, with a series of four plays
on the theme of madness: Crazy For You,
King Lear, A Midsummer Night's Dream, and
Alice Through The Looking Glass, at the
Festival Theatre and the Avon Theatre, with
breakfasts at Balzac's and lunch at Fellini's,
with Cyn, my best friend, writing partner, and
girlfriend from Grade One, Two, Three, Four ....
We had a reunion last summer and went to
Stratford a few times to see a few plays so we
thought we'd book a hotel for a week and see
four plays over five days to keep our reunion
going and going and going ....

2. The Balzac Award For Poetry

Winning the Balzac Award for Poetry changed my
life, a few years ago, filling me with inspiration and
ambition, with a desire to write one hundred books
like Balzac and then one hundred more because
my age is not Balzac's age and we live in the golden
age of computers so I realized Balzac's accomplishment
with a nib pen dipped into ink or coffee was quite
impressive but I could write more than one hundred
books, like Balzac's ouvre, called La Comedie
Humaine, so I wrote 100 books and called it
The Human Comedy then moved to China to
write 100 more, called The Great Wall Of China
Books Series, and my output kept improving,
increasing, expanding, so I wrote thirty books
the year I moved to the Far East and added a few
more when I returned to Canada for the summer:
Dalian: A Long Poem
Toronto: A Very Long Poem
Oh Canada: A Very Long Poem On Canada Day
and one called
Gravenhurst and Bethune and China:
A Long Poem Chronicling A Road Trip From
Toronto To Muskoka And Back Again, or
A Field Guide For Chinese Tourists In Canada,
and now I'm in Stratford, again, staying at
an old hotel, the closest place to Balzac's.
wearing a black Balzac's tee-shirt, in
a place called Balzac's, drinking coffee called
Balzac's Blend, writing about this trip while
surrounded by posters and pictures of
Balzac and I got the unmistakable impression
Balzac joined us for breakfast in the morning
we woke up in Stratford and he stayed
with us as we celebrated a week of summer
at the Stratford Festival with four plays on the
theme of madness at the Festival Theatre and
the Avon in Stratford: Crazy For You,
King Lear, A Midsummer Night's Dream,
and Alice Through The Looking Glass.

3. Jack Kerouac, W.O. Mitchell And Me

I wrote Balzac style, at the start of this
long poem, with a pen on paper, because we
wrote for three or four hours in the morning,
and I finished a long poem called Gravenhurst
and Bethune and China, a kind of field guide for
Chinese visitors to Canada, writing
in Balzac's, with Balzac, and my old MacBook
Pro was down to 3% of its battery life, so I got
that warning: "You are now running on
reserve power" and what can you do after that
except pull out your journal and ballpoint pen
and keep going because, frankly, I feel as though
I'm on fire this summer, this year, the past
half decade, maybe the whole decade, or this
century, this millennium, so far, as I keep
writing faster and finishing book after
book after book in record time and
what about the quality, my friends in China
asked me, but not my bestie in Canada, as
she knows I'm writing literature, I'm
in the zone, as they say, writing like
Kerouac when he wrote the first draft of
On The Road, writing like a novel marathoner
at the Muskoka Novel Marathon, the way
my buddy the Canadian poet Gary Barwin
said he would write inspired by his first
novel marathon, saying, "I'll divide the
rest of the year into three day chunks and
write over 100 books per year", only
it doesn't happen that way, I thought,
but the more you write, the more you
write more, better, and faster at a
marathon inspired by the energy of a
group of writers, but only at a
marathon, or so I thought until
this year when I went to China and
came back to Canada full of energy
and loaded with the desire to write,
with so much to say, and the ability to

do it the way Allen Ginsburgh wrote
Howl, at top speed, full of
education, information, experience,
infatuation, and ambition, ready to
pour it forth the way my main mentor,
W.O. Mitchell, author of Who Has
Seen The Wind, taught us to at the
Banff Centre School Of Fine Arts with
Eli Mandel decades ago and I've been
practicing while teaching others
ever since, giving the Banff experience to
students in high school and summer
school and summer camps and adults
in writing workshops and summer
camp for adults and at poetry and
novel marathons and I'm certain
you can sense the energy I've got
going in these long sentences over
so many lines of free verse poetry
exploding like qi or chi or sexy
life energy shooting through my
meridians out my hands and fingers
onto the page or computer screen
and into your brain and heart so
you feel energized, inspired, and it's
healing, too, and sexy, as all this
energy is the same creative, dynamic,
awe-inspiring, life-affirming, super-
charged life force a bipolar artistic
genius feels in the hypomanic phase.

Am I hypomanic? you ask. Well,
I'm feeling energized, creative,
sexy, excited, inspired, happy,
joyful, blissful, ecstatic every day,
now, and I hope you are, too, reading
this while drinking coffee or maybe
an energy drink like Red Bull, not
that this is an ad for energy drinks
or even coffee, for that matter,
consult with your physician if you

plan to take a lot of caffeine and
go in a novel marathon or write
one hundred books like Balzac or
two hundred or so with me.

do it the way Allen Ginsburgh wrote
Howl, at top speed, full of
education, information, experience,
infatuation, and ambition, ready to
pour it forth the way my main mentor,
W.O. Mitchell, author of Who Has
Seen The Wind, taught us to at the
Banff Centre School Of Fine Arts with
Eli Mandel decades ago and I've been
practicing while teaching others
ever since, giving the Banff experience to
students in high school and summer
school and summer camps and adults
in writing workshops and summer
camp for adults and at poetry and
novel marathons and I'm certain
you can sense the energy I've got
going in these long sentences over
so many lines of free verse poetry
exploding like qi or chi or sexy
life energy shooting through my
meridians out my hands and fingers
onto the page or computer screen
and into your brain and heart so
you feel energized, inspired, and it's
healing, too, and sexy, as all this
energy is the same creative, dynamic,
awe-inspiring, life-affirming, super-
charged life force a bipolar artistic
genius feels in the hypomanic phase.

Am I hypomanic? you ask. Well,
I'm feeling energized, creative,
sexy, excited, inspired, happy,
joyful, blissful, ecstatic every day,
now, and I hope you are, too, reading
this while drinking coffee or maybe
an energy drink like Red Bull, not
that this is an ad for energy drinks
or even coffee, for that matter,
consult with your physician if you

plan to take a lot of caffeine and
go in a novel marathon or write
one hundred books like Balzac or
two hundred or so with me.

4. A Blast From The Past

Here's the story that was the winner of the
Balzac Award for Poetry. (It's a prose poem.)

Balzac In Stratford

A lover always thinks of his mistress first and
himself second; with a husband it runs the other
way, Balzac once said.
I discovered that was true on summer in Stratford.
We used to meet for coffee at the tiny back deck of
Balzac's Coffee, downtown, after classes.
We were both taking a summer course that included
seeing all the plays in Stratford ....
Everybody in the course said the same thing: It's so
nice you two could meet again and have a reunion over
the summer in Stratford and go to all the plays together.
But we met there, in that course, for the first time.
We took her kids to the costume warehouse and we had
a blast.
She left the kids with her parents, who lived there,
sometimes, so she could meet me for coffee.
Surrounded by mature trees and vines, Balzac's deck
proved to be the perfect place for a romantic rendez-vous.
It was her idea. Honest. She's the one who told me
about Balzac's.
"Don't forget to look up on the way through, she said.
"Original moulded tin ceilings and a display of
vintage coffee ads and tins are part of the decor,
and the ambiance."
Of course, there was also the 12-kilo micro-roaster.
Balzac's selection of coffee beans from around the
world were roasted right there and gave the cafe a
heavenly aroma. While I waited for her out back,
on the deck, I read some more Balzac.
I was working on his magnum opus, the sequence of
100 novels, stories, and plays called La Comedie humaine.
I liked his characters. They're so multi-faceted.
Even his lesser characters are complex, morally

ambiguous, and fully human.
Inanimate objects are imbued with character, as well, in Balzac.
Paris, the backdrop for much of his writing, is like a character, in his stories.
His work made me think about Proust, Zola, Dickens, Dostoyevsky, Henry James, Faulkner, Kerouac, and Calvino, as well as Engels.
Mostly, it made me think of La Comedie Humaine.
It turned out the woman I was in love with was not free.
She was married, with children.
But the kids loved me.
She said her husband was a brute and the kids agreed.
"I'll leave him," she said. "And after some time on my own, I'll be ready for a better relationship with you."
But, as Balzac said, A mother who is really a mother is never free.
That wonderful woman never managed to extricate herself from her marriage.
Well, not yet, anyway.
Every summer, I return to Stratford, return to Balzac's Coffee, return to Balzac's back deck, and I wait for her to return to me.
It has been ten years.
Her kids will be out of school and on their own, before too long.
I'm still waiting.
I'll wait forever.
Balzac waited a long time for his love.
After waiting for eighteen years, Balzac finally married Ewelina Hanska, his longtime love, and then he died, five months later.
It's like the great love story in the Latin American magical realist novel by Laura Esquival called Like Water For Chocolate.
She introduced me to her sister, at Balzac's, but I wasn't interested in that scenario.
I was in love with her.
I loved Stratford, too, but never so much as that summer. And I loved Balzac, too, and I keep reading

his magnum opus, but I'm still not finished with
The Human Comedy.
5. Stratford, Canada

There is nothing like Stratford
anywhere else in the world but
maybe China could copy it, build
a replica someplace, maybe
the JinShiTan or Golden
Pebble Beach part of Dalian, in
Dongbei, or north-east China,
where I live ....

Stratford is a city on the
Avon River in Perth County in
southwestern Ontario, Canada,
with a population of 30,000 and
when the area was first settled
by Europeans, back in 1832,
the townsite and the river were
named after Stratford-upon-Avon,
England, and it was the seat of
Perth County, and the swan
became a symbol of the city, so
each year twenty-four white swans
and two black swans are
released into the Avon River and
the town is now famous for
being the home of the
Stratford Shakespeare Festival
with four theatres featuring
Shakespeare at the Festival Theatre
and the Tom Patterson Theatre and
musicals at the Avon and new
Canadian plays at the Studio Theatre.

Ahhhh Stratford! Few places in
Ontario are lovelier or more alive
with culture and character than
Stratford, a charming Victorian city
nestled in pastoral countryside

a few short hours from Toronto
and the U.S.A. – a destination
internationally renowned as
one of North America's greatest
arts towns. It is a vibrant creative
culture, expressed by its famous
theatre company, celebrated in
music, the innovative cuisine of
its restaurants and it is also a
garden city landscaped with
well-conserved Victorian architecture.

It is best to visit for a few days,
staying in one of the elegant hotels or
intimate inns or bed and breakfasts –
from the comfy cottages to luxurious
heritage mansions. I picked an
old hotel close to Balzac's, right
behind Filini's, around the corner
from the Avon and the Studio
theatres, and a short walk from
the Festival Theatre and the
Tom Patterson and the Avon River.

The Stratford Festival, formerly known as
the Stratford Shakespearean and then
Shakespeare Festival, is an
internationally recognized annual celebration of
theatre, running from April to October in
the Canadian city of Stratford, Ontario.
Theatre-goers, actors, and playwrights flock to
Stratford to take part — many of the greatest
Canadian, British, and American actors
take roles at the Stratford festival.
It was one of the first and is still one of the most
prominent arts festivals in Canada and is
recognized worldwide for its productions of
Shakespearean plays.

The Festival's primary mandate is
to present productions of William Shakespeare's plays

but it also produces a wide variety of theatre
from Greek tragedy to contemporary works.
Shakepeare's work typically represents
about a third of the Festival's offerings.

The success of the festival dramatically changed
the image of Stratford into one of a city where
the arts and tourism play important roles in
its economy. The festival attracts many tourists
from outside Canada, mainly British and American,
and is seen as a very important part of
Stratford's tourism sector.

Well known actors who have participated in
the festival include Alan Bates, Brian Bedford,
Douglas Campbell, Len Cariou, Brent Carver,
Hume Cronyn, Brian Dennehy, Colm Feore,
Megan Follows, Lorne Greene, Paul Gross,
Uta Hagen, Julie Harris, Martha Henry,
William Hutt, James Mason, Eric McCormack,
Loreena McKennitt, Richard Monette, John Neville,
Nicholas Pennell, Amanda Plummer, Christopher
Plummer, Sarah Polley, Douglas Rain, Kate Reid,
Jason Robards, Paul Scofield, William Shatner,
Maggie Smith, Jessica Tandy, Peter Ustinov and
Al Waxman.

Alec Guinness and Irene Worth were in the cast of
Stratford's inaugural performance of Richard III in
1953. A young, unknown Christopher Walken appeared in
Stratford's 1968 stage productions of Romeo and Juliet and
A Midsummer's Night Dream, portraying
Romeo and Lysander respectively.

The Festival was founded as the
Stratford Shakespearean Festival of Canada, due mainly to
Tom Patterson, a Stratford-native journalist who
wanted to revitalize his town's economy by
creating a theatre festival dedicated to
the works of William Shakespeare, as
the town shares the name of Shakespeare's birthplace.

Stratford was a railway junction and major
locomotive shop, and was facing a disastrous loss of
employment with the imminent elimination of
steam power. British actor and director
Tyrone Guthrie agreed to become the festival's first
Actor Alec Guinness spoke the first lines of
the first play produced by the festival:
"Now is the winter of our discontent / Made glorious summer ...."

This first performance took place in a giant canvas tent on
the banks of the River Avon. The season comprised
just two plays: Richard III and All's Well That Ends Well.
In the second year the playbill expanded, and included
the first non-Shakespeare play, Oedipus Rex.
The Festival Theatre was opened in 1957, and was
deliberately designed to resemble a tent, in memory of
those first performances. The Festival Theatre's thrust stage was
designed by to resemble both a classic Greek amphitheatre and
Shakespeare's Globe Theatre, and has become
a model for other stages in North America and Great Britain.

The Festival runs from April to October, and has
four permanent venues: the Festival Theatre,
the Avon Theatre, the Tom Patterson Theatre, and
the Studio Theatre. Its season playbills usually include
a variety of classical and contemporary works
and at least one musical.

The Stratford Festival Forum runs during the season and
features music concerts, readings by major authors,
lectures, and discussions with actors or management.

The line-up for the summer of 2014 was great:
King Lear – by William Shakespeare
Crazy for You – lyrics by Ira Gershwin, music by George Gershwin
A Midsummer Night's Dream – by William Shakespeare
The Beaux' Stratagem – by George Farquhar
Hay Fever – by Noël Coward
Man of La Mancha –
Alice Through the Looking Glass – by Lewis Carroll,
adapted by James Reaney

Mother Courage – by Bertolt Brecht
King John – by William Shakespeare
Antony and Cleopatra – by William Shakespeare
Christina, The Girl King – by Michel Marc Bouchard

While I was in China, on the other side of the planet,
I got tickets online for King Lear,
Crazy For You, A Midsummer Night's Dream, and
Alice Through The Looking Glass.

6. Relationships

My sister the relationship counsellor
has retired from her second career
and is on a trip around the world so
she's in Canada for a few weeks and
we had a reunion at my brother's
place up by Penetanguishine near
Balm Beach on Georgian Bay at the
north end of Wasaga Beach, the
longest freshwater beach in the world,
which we love, with the Blue Mountains
as a backdrop, and the three of us
spent a long afternoon at a little beach
down the road that is not as crowded
as the more famous places and we
had time to talk, really talk, so of course
she asked me about my relationship with
Cyn and with other women in my
life in the past as that's her favourite
thing to talk about, so I told her,
again, We're just friends, old friends,
having a reunion after decades after
being boyfriend and girlfriend in
Grade One, Two, Three, Four, so
she said, Are you friends, or are you
friends with benefits?
She says that relationships these days
fall into different categories ranging
from friends to lovers to married and
there's lots of categories for each of
those categories and what she wanted
to know was if we are friends and lovers
going to get married or are we
friends with benefits or
friends with some benefits or
friends with limited benefits or
friends with very limited benefits so
I told her her categories sounded kinda
crazy to me so she asked me for
details, she always wants the details,

lots of details, so I told her we are
affectionate and loving but she
insisted on details so I told her
Cyn loves my
foot rubs, frequently, and
sometimes the foot rub turns into
a leg rub, and occassionaly that leads
to a neck rub with a shoulder massage
and we kissed one night at
Stratford, last year, but it was
a little like kissing your sister,
if you know what I mean,
not that I've ever kissed my
sister, and, let's face it, I'm a
a man, a lusty man, getting
ancient but feeling like a
much younger kind of guy,
last year a Canadian doctor told me
I was going to die soon but my
Chinese doctor says I'm
healthy and strong as a
twenty-four-year-old and
after a lot of Traditional
Chinese Medicine in China
I've got a lot of chi flowing
through my meridians and
life force energy is the same as
sexual energy is the same as
creative energy so I am
spending a lot of time with my
former girlfriend and we're
quite close and I'm now
writing more and faster and
better than ever, which is
really saying something, so
she said, I get it, even if
you're not getting any, and she
laughed hard at her own joke
and at my situation because
she senses I would like to
deepen the relationship,

as we used to say, and my
brother said, Yeah, you'd like
to deepen it about .... But I
cut him off before he said
anything embarrassing and
suggested we all go jump in
the lake, again, and we all
got up from our place on the
beach to wade into the water
and then dive in and swim
the way we did at Gull Lake
Park decades ago when we
lived in Gravenhurst and
I thought about my doctor
in China, advising me against
swimming in cold water, to
take care of my back, my spine,
my health, as she believes
all of Canada is a cold country
and Canadians need to heat up
their internal organs, as
Traditional Chinese Medicine is
not all about germs and drugs
and surgery, it's about hot and
cold and balance and energy
so I let my brother and sister
swim like fish in the cold water
while I waded back to the beach to
do qigung in the sunshine until
the water warmed up enough
for me to go swimming, if
you know what I mean, maybe
that's a good metaphor for
a relationship or the perfect
objective correlative for a
contemporary romance with
an old friend you feel
close to and very attracted to
and you think is gorgeous
and so does everyone else
as she is a beautiful woman

with blonde hair and
Pamela Anderson's
measurements and
sometimes us guys need to be
reminded that it's not all about
what Freud said we
think about every
seven seconds and I've always
thought Freud was a little
oversexed or maybe obsessed
with sex because I think about
a lot of other things and every
decade or so my ability to
concentrate on other things has
jumped up impressively so
while my sister was asking me about
levels of friendship and benefits
I was thinking about world peace
and global warming and international
politics and this idea I have about
cleaning up the Pacific Ocean,
collecting all the plastic floating in
the Pacific Vortex and recycling it into
big plastic floating ice floe replicas
for polar bears to rest on while
fishing or hunting for seals in the
Arctic and the fake ice floes could
reflect the sun's rays to stop
the Arctic melting and global
warming, reverse the trend, so the
Arctic freezes over again and the
oceans stop rising so
my place on the coast of China
is safe again and everybody on
Earth can relax a bit on the
condition everybody remembers
the warning that comes with
global warming and we stop
polluting the planet like we have
another one to go to
and my sister says

that's not what you're really
thinking about and
man, you've got it bad, if
that's what you think you're
thinking about! So I tell her
she should take another
swim in the cold water of
Georgian Bay.

It was great to see my sister
again after such a long time
and I wished her well on the
rest of her trip around the
planet. Bon voyage! I said.
Bon voyage! Hate to see you
go! as I headed back to
Toronto so I could pick up
Cyn and go to Stratford for
a week with four plays, and
my sister said, did you say
foreplay, or four plays, so
I laughed and said, Bon
voyage, again.Stratford And China

Note: China copies things it loves
and it should be seen as a form of
flattery or appreciation as that is
the ancient culture of China that is
misunderstood in the current era
and you should think again if you
think China copies for other reasons.

Listen to me, getting defensive
about China, like China needs me
to stick up for it, that huge country
with 1.4 billion people, the next
superpower, taking over from
the U.S.A. during the decline of
the American Empire. I think.

When I think about Canada's place

in the world, a little bit above
the U.S.A., as we like to say,
the way Muskoka is a little bit above
Toronto, the way Scotland is
a bit above England, I think about
Stratford, which is proudly
Canadian, but the Stratford Festival is
mostly Shakespearean, and my
connection to this place isn't very
multi-cultural, like Canada, it
connects me to my ancestral past
in England, where the Averys
came from, in and around Averbury,
down the road from Stonehenge,
and my more recent connections
to England and Stratford as
I became a drama teacher after
a few years of teaching English at
high school as the drama teacher was
retiring and wanted me to take over
and I went to a long weekend workshop
with Robert Bly, down in Peterborough,
at Trent University, and came back ready
to teach drama, as Bly helped me
touch the wildman, as we used to say,
back in the day, when Bly was the leader of
the men's movement, which was growing
up alongside the women's movement, and
after teaching drama for a year I went
back to school to study drama, starting
with an Honours Specialist in English in
England, at the Herstmonceux Campus of
Queen's University, at Herstmonceux
Castle, which included a lot of drama, and
then I spent two summers, two great and
glorious summers in Stratford, in the
AQ course, for Additional Qualifications in
Drama, like getting another undergraduate
degree, at the Stratford Campus of the
U of T, one summer, and UT/OISE
the next summer, and we had to see

all the plays in Stratford, those summers,
what a hardship, what a way to study
drama, as well as do course work, and go to
theatre talks and discussions and luncheons
to meet the directors, producers, actors,
artistic director, carpenters, everybody, and
tour backstage and the costume warehouse,
and work with other teachers, something
I love, and discovered drama teachers are
even more fun than English teachers, and
the way I remember it the sun was always
shining, those summers in Stratford, and
then I felt inspired to teach more drama and
take a summer job as Program Director for
Theatre at an international arts camp down
near Niagara Falls, called Centauri, where
we wrote and produced plays in just
ten days, and my favourite was a
production I wrote an outline for and got
my talented drama kids to fill in called
Shakespeare's Women, based on an idea
one of my first Writers Craft students
came up with when she said, I wish
Shakespeare was still alive -- so I could
kill him, which struck me as being
brilliant, and in my play each of the
actors had to pick a character, one of
Shakespeare's women, and bring them to
life with a monologue and together we
created dialogue so each had a
conversation with Shakespeare and then
they killed him so picture a stage with
tombstones and fog, to start the play,
and Shakespeare wandering around the
graveyard, carrying a skull, and touching
the tombstones or the permanently
sleeping bodies of Juliet and Ophelia
and Viola and several others so
each one came alive and then they all
ganged up on the bard and it was all about
the idea that Shakespeare was not a man

but all those plays with great female
characters and great insight into the
psyche of women must have been written
by several women rather than just
one man, and the play was a huge
hit, each time I did it, and that remains
the biggest hit I've had as a playwright,
although I also got a group of
Gravenhurst drama kids to write a play
based on one of my short short stories,
called Mini-Marts, and we took it on
the road for the Theatre In The Community
course, connected to our Writers Craft
course, and toured around to all the
schools in our board, which covered a
big area, called Trillium Lakelands,
all over Central Ontario, with
The Story Store, about going to a
convenience store to get a story and
getting the order mixed up so
stories got mashed together and
the little kids in the audiences loved to see
high school kids mixing up their
favourite fairy tales and other stories
and that was another big hit like
the time I had a poetry club called
The Semi-Dead Poets at my first
school, Grey Highlands, over in
Flesherton, in the Beaver Valley,
south of Owen Sound, in case you never
heard of Flesherton, and we toured
around to do poetry writing workshops
at the local elementary schools and
it was great to see the little kids treat
high school poets like rock stars
just like the Gravenhurst drama kids
and the drama kids at Centauri,
and it all came out of my summers in
Stratford, plus my summer in
England, at Herstmonceux Castle,
and those places are connected in my

mind with the Banff Centre School of
Fine Arts where I learned all about
freefall or freewriting or
Mitchell's Messy Method with
W.O. Mitchell and the poet
Eli Mandel and that's what I'm
teaching now in Dalian, China, for
Maple Leaf International Schools,
using the B.C. curriculum, and it's also
inspiring my novel marathons, with
the Muskoka Novel Marathon now
in its 14th season and this summer
we are launching the Toronto
Novel Marathon and maybe
there will be a China Novel Marathon
someday in the future.

What a life, I often say, to myself.
What a dream, as Deepak Chopra
taught me to say. He said, If you
meditate every day, your life will be
like a dream, like mine, and he
made me think of the old song,
Row row row your boat / life is
like a dream, which is a theme
Shakespeare sometimes used and
I had to study meditation for
several years at a place called
The Zen Forest, in the Far East of
Ontario, in the country north of
Belleville, as the poet Al Purdy
used to say, before I could really
get the dream going, but once it
got going it got better and better,
as an older writer friend of mine
used to say -- The better it gets,
the better it gets. And that's the way
it goes these days, thank G-d, thank
the higher powers, thank my
lucky stars, as I cultivate the
attitude of gratitude and keep on

working on enlightenment and keep writing and returning to Stratford for the theatre festival with Cyn.

The Balzac Channel

"Who was Balzac?" Cyn says.
She was an actress and she likes to read
murder mysteries but loves
Shakespeare on the stage, so
I tell her Balzac was a French writer
in the 1800s best known
for producing an enormous body of
novels describing virtually every
aspect of life in Paris and the
French provinces. These novels
were collectively called the
"Comédie Humaine" or
Human Comedy, and
Balzac completed about
90 of them, out of the 150 or so
he planned to write.

"Only 90?" Cyn says.
You see why I love her.
"You wrote more than that
before you moved to China,"
she says proudly. "You wrote
100 here and you're writing
another 100 there. And
Balzac is so famous for
writing 100, but he only
finished 90?"

"You rock," I tell her.

"What did he write about?"
she wanted to know. "Did he
write about the big themes
- love and death - like you?"

I told her that the better-known
works in the Comédie—such as
Old Goriot and Lost Illusions
—are studies of youthfulness,

ambition, and the power of money.

"Love and death are more ambitious
themes," Cyn says. "You could
write about power and money --
in China," she added.

Those themes dominate Balzac's
work, I tell her, and they
give the Comédie a certain unity.
But Balzac was well aware that his
sweeping attempt to chronicle
the French world he lived in
inevitably had a lot of holes.
"Paris is an ocean," he wrote. "Throw
in the plummet, you will never reach
bottom. Survey it; describe it.
However conscientious your survey
and careful your chart, however
numerous and concerned to learn
the truth the explorers of this sea
may be, there will always be
a virgin realm, an unknown cavern,
flowers, pearls, monsters, things
undreamed of, overlooked by
the literary divers."

"Didn't you write a book about
Balzac?" Cyn says. "A book of poetry?
What was it called? 'What Balzac
Said'?"

Yes, I said, I channeled Balzac and
chatted with him, showed him what
life in Canada and the contemporary
world is like now, in the new
millennium.

"Can you still do that?" she said.
"Channel Balzac?"

"Maybe," I said. "Let me give it
a shot."

We were in Balzac's in Stratford.
She was drinking an Americano with
three shots and I was enjoying a
cafe mocha. "Let me get you a
shot or two or three added to your
mocha," she suggested.

Hi, I said, I'm Balzac. I was born in
Tours, in France, at the end of the
1700s.

Hey, Balzac, Cyn said. Tell me
a bit about yourself.

Well, Balzac said, my father came from
peasant stock but rose up through society
and established himself as a middle-class
civil servant by the time I was born.

Interesting, she said. My friend Martin is
a writer. He was born in Bracebridge, Muskoka,
Ontario, Canada, in the middle of the
20th century. Both his parents'
families came from peasant stock in
Scotland and England, a generation or two
earlier. His father and his father's father
were war heroes, in the First World War and
the Second World War, but
the war ruined them.
And after the war, his father became
a civil servant, like yours,
shortly after the time he was born.

Balzac looked uninterested and he
sounded disinterested. "My mother was
thirty-one years younger than my father,"
he said. "I remembered her as a stingingly
unaffectionate parent. She sent me away to

boarding school at age eight ...."

Marty's mother was a saint, Cyn said.
She was very loving and we remember her as
a great mother and a fabulous human being.
All our old friends remember her that way, too.

Balzac's disinterest was consistent.
My family moved to Paris, he said, where I
worked as a legal clerk but then abandoned
a career in law in order to pursue a life in
literature.

Cyn was equally persistend.
Marty was a Poly Sci major in first year
of university, in Victoria, B.C., and was
thinking about going to law school, but picked
literature over law, she said.

Balzac kept talking about himself.
I kept myself afloat by
writing popular journalism and
sensationalistic fiction, using
pseudonyms.

Marty is a journalist and he's written
a million articles for newspapers and
magazines plus books that are
biographies of Olympic athletes who
were Canadian and world champions.

Balzac shrugged. My idea was
to write the history so many
historians have neglected --
that of Manners -- took shape in
the early 1830s and the term
"Comédie Humaine" came into use in
1842.

Cyn rolled her eyes but Balzac
did not catch her.

"I used the series name
'Studies of Nineteenth Century Manners'
before then," Balzac said.

We could call my friend's books
Studies In Late Twentieth Century
And Early Twenty-First Century
Manners, instead of
The Human Comedy and
The Great Wall Of China Books,
Cyn said.

Balzac said, "I retroactively
grouped many of my novels in
the Comédie, presenting
approximately two thousand
characters, and the critics
said that even the most minor
character was well-rounded,
not thin or flat ....

"My gallery of social types," Balzac
went on, included
a few recurring characters who were
modelled loosely on mself
—such as Lucien Chardon,
the over-sensitive young writer
who stars in Lost Illusions, and
Eugène de Rastignac, the
conflicted law student who
plays a major role in Old Goriot.

"That's so interesting," Cyn said flatly,
exercising the Canadian penchant for
irony.

"In order to devote myself to writing,"
Balzac said, "I tended to sleep during
the day and work at night. I also drank

enormous amounts of black coffee
to keep myself alert."

"Marty works full-time as a teacher and
he doesn't drink coffee unless he's with
me in Toronto and we go to Starbucks or
we're in Stratford, where we go to Balzac's."

Do they have anything to eat, here? Balzac
wanted to know. Did you hear about my love
affair? he asked. For ten years, I carried on
an affair with Laure de Berny, a mother of nine
who was twice my age, when we met. And
when that romance collapsed, I formed a bond with
a Ukrainian countess named Eveline Hanska.
After almost two decades, we finally got married
and then .... I don't know what happened ....

Balzac's voice trailed off as he tried to recall
the events of the last year of your life.

You died the same year, Cyn told him bluntly.

Oh? Balzac said. Oh well.

What about my legacy? he wanted to know.
I dunno, Cyn said. Marty might know.

Balzac influenced many of the most important
writers in the history of the modern novel—
including Gustave Flaubert, Henry James,
Marcel Proust, and others, including
Émile Zola, Charles Dickens, Edgar Allan Poe,
Dostoyevsky, Gustave Flaubert,
William Faulkner, Jack Kerouac, and
Italo Calvino, and philosophers, including
Marx and Engels. Henry James wrote about him
in a book called "The Lesson of Balzac"

But today, Balzac is best known for his big
authorial persona than for any specific

contributions to the art of fiction.
The sculptures of Balzac by Auguste Rodin
helped fix the idea of a vigorous, earthy,
imposing Balzac in the public imagination.

Yeah, Cyn said. I saw a picture of one of his
sculptures. It's on a poster in the bathroom.

Balzac was a French novelist and playwright
whose magnum opus was a sequence of
short stories and novels collectively called
La Comédie humaine, or The Human Comedy,
which presents a panorama of French life in
the years after the fall of Napoleon Bonaparte.

Balzac is regarded as one of the founders of
realism in European literature. He is renowned for
his multifaceted characters, who are
morally ambiguous.

What does that mean? Cyn said. 'Morally
ambiguous.' Like Walter White, on
Breaking Bad? Tony Soprano of
The Sopranos? Don Draper in Mad Men?

Balzac would like them, I said.

Were his books long or short? Cyn wanted to know.
Many of his novels were serialized, like Dickens'.
Lost Illusions was a thousand pages but
The Girl with the Golden Eyes was only fifty pages.

How did he write all those books? Cyn asked.
Balzac's work habits are legendary, but
he did not work quickly, I told her. He
worked hard, they say, with incredible
focus and dedication. His preferred
writing process included eating
a light meal in the afternoon,
sleeping until midnight, then getting up and
writing for hours, fuelled by coffee,

lots of black coffee. He would work for
fifteen hours or more at a stretch. He claimed
he once worked for 48 hours straight.

Is that why you made the Balzac Award
for the Muskoka Novel Marathon a
coffee cup trophy given to the writer who
spends the most time working during
the marathon.

Yes, I said, and that reminds me of
Mo Yan, who wrote a novel in Chinese
using the traditional brush and ink on
paper, and completed a book called
Life and Death Are Wearing Me Out
in only 42 days. -- How I wish I could
get Mo Yan in a novel marathon in
China, or get him to come to the
Toronto Novel Marathon, I said.

Too bad you couldn't bring back Balzac
for the Toronto Novel Marathon, Cyn said,
sounding a little less than 100 percent sincere.

You know, I said, many of his works have been
made into popular films, I said.
Name one, Cyn said.
Well, I said, the Chinese author Dai Sijie
published a book called Balzac et la Petite
Tailleuse Chinoise, or Balzac and the
Little Chinese Seamstress and it was
made into a film with the same name
which was pretty popular.

He seems heavy, Cyn said. Dark and
heavy. -- Don't channel him anymore,
okay? she said. I agree but his presence
lingered at the coffee shop in Stratford
named after him and it felt as though
he was with us when we went to see
the plays I had booked while I was in

China, starting with Crazy For You.

7. Crazy for You

After breakfast with Balzac, we went to
Fellini's for lunch, another restaurant in
Stratford, just down the street, called
Ontario Street, and Cyn was a little worried
Fellini would join us for lunch, the way
Balzac joined us for breakfast.

Federico Fellini was an Italian film director and
scriptwriter known for his distinct style that
blends fantasy and baroque images with earthiness.
He is considered one of the most influential
filmmakers of the 20th century, and is widely revered.
In a career spanning almost fifty years, Fellini won
five Academy Awards including
the most Oscars in history for Best
Foreign Language Film.

Some of Fellini's greatest hits were
La Dolce Vita
Boccaccio '70
8½
Giulietta degli spiriti
Satyricon
Roma
Amarcord
Il Casanova di Federico Fellini

What would Balzac have to say to Fellini?
I wondered. What would Fellini say to
Balzac? -- Can't we just eat in peace,
Cyn said. The two of us. Without this
trip to Stratford turning into
Midnight In Paris or Night In The Museum
or something terrible like that?

How strange to have Balzac and
Fellini connected by Ontario Street
in Stratford, on the same block,
Cyn said. I love this place.

After breakfast at Balzac's and
lunch at Fellini's we went to the
Festival Theatre to see
The New Gershwin Musical
with music and lyrics by
George Gershwin and Ira Gershwin,
book by Ken Ludwig, a Co-Conception by
Ken Ludwig and Mike Ockrent,
inspired by material by Guy Bolton and
John McGowan, originally produced
on Broadway by Roger Horchow and
Elizabeth William, directed and
choreographed by Donna Feore for
the Stratford production in 2014.

What's it about? I asked Cyn.
She said, It's about this guy
named Bobby Child who is
sent to Deadrock, Nevada to
foreclose on a derelict theatre but
the banker, Child, falls for
the theatre owner's daughter,
Polly Baker, and they use
the theatre to put on a show
to try to save the place.

Sounds familiar, I said.
Yeah, she said. Can he reconcile
the demands of duty and love –
and his own dreams of dancing?

Who's who in this big shoe? I asked.
BOBBY CHILD is a young man in love
with musical theater
BELA ZANGLER is a producer
LANK HAWKINSN has a saloon in Nevada
EVERETT BAKER is Polly's father who is
lost in memories of his wife on stage
POLLY BAKER is the singing postmistress and
"All American Girl"

IRENE ROTH is a New York Society debutant
EUGENE FODOR is an English tourist and so is
his wife, or is it his sister, PATRICIA FODOR
MOTHER (Mrs. Lottie Child) is Bobby's
business-oriented and controlling parent
and there are 10 FOLLIES GIRLS who
sing and dance as well as 10 COWBOYS
who sing and learn how to dance, motivated
by the Follies Girls

What are the big songs in the show?
I asked her. "I Got Rhythm"?
Yes, she said. And also
"Nice Work if You Can Get It" and
"Someone to Watch Over Me" and
lots more. It's billed as
"The New Gershwin Musical Comedy"
but it is based on an old musical called
Girl Crazy with songs from
several other productions as well.
"K-ra-zy for You" (from Treasure Girl)
"I Can't Be Bothered Now" (from A Damsel in Distress)
"Bidin' My Time" (from Girl Crazy)
"Things Are Looking Up" (from A Damsel in Distress)
"Could You Use Me" (from Girl Crazy)
"Shall We Dance?" (from Shall We Dance)
"Slap That Bass" (from Shall We Dance)
"Embraceable You" (from Girl Crazy)
"I Got Rhythm" (from Girl Crazy)
"The Real American Folk Song is a Rag" (from Ladies First)
"What Causes That?" (from Treasure Girl)
"Naughty Baby" and
"Nice Work If You Can Get It" (from A Damsel in Distress)

That's quite a list, I said. It sounds like
poetry, to me.
What were the reviews like? I asked her.
Cyn read some of them to me.

"A rollicking, rhythmic, delight"
"a full out celebration of dance"

"This summer's market for snappy, satisfying
musical entertainment has just been filled
and filled beautifully"
"a resounding, unqualified hit, which ranks as
the finest choreographed musical ever to
appear on a Stratford stage."
"a shot of adrenaline"
"triumphant"
"the audience, fed by the energy of the number,
won't stop applauding"
"lots of comedic one-liners and
plenty of spectacular dancing"
"Stratford's production has it all,
the songs, superb actors and acting and
dancing that will knock your socks off!"
"Stratford captures magic that made
'Crazy for You' a Broadway smash"

We loved it, like everyone else, and loved
out seats, in the front row. We were backstage at
the Zangler Theater in New York City in
the 1930s during a performance of the "Zangler Follies."

The play started before the play started with some
action on stage before the opening in the wings and
on the stage of Zangler's Broadway Theater with
a show is in progress and, in the wings,
STAGEHANDS were working the lights,
a STAGE MANAGER was calling cues, and
as the curtain rises, TESS, the Dance Director, is
drilling four SHOW GIRLS in a short routine.
We soon discover Impresario Bela Zangler
was in love with Tess, his Dance Director, but
Zangler was married, so
Tess rejects his advances. Also backstage is
Bobby Child, heir to a wealthy banking family, who
yearns to be in show business. Bobby talks Zangler into
letting him audition but bombs.
Outside the theatre, Bobby is accosted by Irene,
his wealthy fiance, whom he doesn't want to marry,
then by his mother who insists that he go to

Deadrock, Nevada to foreclose on a property.
As the women argue and harangue Bobby, he escapes by
conjuring up the Follies Girls but when
Bobby returns to reality, he chooses Deadrock over
Irene and hurries off to Grand Central Station.

Three days later we're in Deadrock, a
has-been mining town. The only woman in
town is Polly Baker, the fiesty postmistress.
Her father, Everett, owns the Gaiety Theater,
a grand old Victorian structure that has
gone to seed. A letter arrives from New York
stating that a banker named Bobby Child
has been sent to foreclose on the theatre if
Everett fails to meet his mortgage payments.
Polly vows that if she ever meets this
"Bobby Child" she'll do "something ugly!"
Moments later, Bobby staggers into town, sees
Polly, falls in love with her and sings
Things Are Looking Up.

Polly, beneath her brash exterior, yearns
for a man she can love, so she sings
Someone To Watch Over Me.

The town's saloon is owned by Lank Hawkins,
who wants to marry Polly and buy Everett's theater.
Inside the saloon, Polly meets Bobby
for the first time, and Bobby declares
his love for her, singing Could You Use Me?

Polly is unimpressed with his Eastern ways, but
Bobby urges her to "have her fling" and
teaches her to dance. As they swirl through
the desert, Polly falls deeply in love with Bobby
while they sing Shall We Dance?

That night, on the stage of the Gaiety Theater,
Bobby gets a great idea: They can save the theater by
putting on a show!
After Polly is persuaded to join in the plan,

Bobby introduces himself:
"I'm Bobby Child" he says.
The name sinks in and Polly slaps him
across the face.

Heartbroken, Polly flees in tears, never
wanting to see him again.
Bobby, too, is heartbroken but suddenly,
spying a trunk of costumes, he gets
another idea: "Bela Zangler!"

Three days later, ten glamorous Follies Girls
who are Bobby's old friends arrive in Deadrock to
the amazement of the menfolk.
Along with the girls is Bobby masquerading as
Zangler, complete with beard, cane and
Hungarian accent. He's been sent, he says, by
Bobby Child.

Polly and Everett readily agree to
let the great impresario put on a show to
save the theatre.

Two weeks later, preparations for the show are
in full swing but the men are still disastrous performers,
but "Zangler" (i.e. Bobby) changes all that
in the course of a single rehearsal as
they sing Slap That Bass.

Irene shows up, looking for Bobby.
She recognizes him and threatens to
expose him to Polly if he doesn't promise to
return with her to New York.
When Irene leaves, "Zangler" tries
to persuade Polly to give Bobby a chance but
Polly confesses that she's madly in love with
"Zangler."
Bobby is horrified and sings Embraceable You.

The following evening, the cast prepares for the show
singing Tonight's the Night, but Lank is desperate to

stop the show and Irene is desperate to
find Bobby, but when people are spotted coming
from the station, the cast assembles on the street but
the only arrivals are an English couple -- the Fodors
-- who are writing a guidebook to the American West.

The company has now hit rock bottom, and Zangler is
the most desolate of all. He apologizes for failing but
as he starts to leave, Polly speaks up.
So what if they didn't sell any tickets?
Since "Zangler" came along, something magical happened.
The whole town has been working together,
caring for each other, and "feeling alive!" so
they sing I Got Rhythm.

As despair turns to celebration,
the real Zangler staggers into town but
nobody notices him for a while.

Bobby, his time is running out, asks Polly to
marry him, but she turns him down, confessing
that she's in love with "Zangler" so
he explains that he is "Zangler" but
she doesn't believe him- and
as he tries to convince her,
the real Zangler staggers in.
As Polly kisses Zangler with passion,
Bobby grabs a bottle of booze and leaves.
When Polly leaves, Zangler explains to
Tess that his wife left him and that
he came to Deadrock to be with her.
Suddenly she gets an idea:
he is Zangler, and could save the theatre!
As an experienced producer, he'd know how to
advertise and sell tickets. When Zangler refuses,
Tess walks off.

Zangler gets drunk and Bobby, also drunk,
dressed as "Zangler"
to prove to Polly that he wasn't lying
joins the real Zangler and

the two Zanglers bemoan
the loss of their women
singing What Causes That?

Polly sees the two Zanglers out cold
under the table and realizes
Bobby was telling the truth. But
instead of loving him for it, she's
storms out of the saloon.

Irene realizes she and Lank are soul mates so
she wastes no time in seducing him by
singing Naughty Baby.
The Fodors sing Stiff Upper Lip,
Polly is no longer angry with Bobby but
to Bobby and Polly's amazement,
the decision of the company is to give up so
Bobby says goodbye to Polly, says he is
going back to New York but Polly is
shocked and when Bobby hints he would
stay for her sake, Polly is too proud to
admit that she loves him so she sings
They Can't Take That Away From Me and
Bobby leaves so Polly sings But Not For Me.

Suddenly, Zangler sweeps into the theatre,
writes check after check to pay for a new show,
confesses to Tess that
although the "cowboys" are good dancers,
he's really doing it all for her.
He truly loves her.
Tess, for once is speechless.

Meanwhile, in New York, Bobby is
trying to be a banker, singing New York Interlude but
all he can think about is Polly and Deadrock.
His mother has foreclosed on the Zangler Theater and
gives him the deed but when Bobby learns
Zangler lost the property by
"wasting all his money on that theatre in Nevada"
- all for Tess's sake - he's suddenly reminded that

money is transitory and only love matters so
he sings Nice Work If You Can Get It and
heads for Deadrock.

Lank and Irene are happily married and
singing Bidin' My Time, the theatre is playing to
full houses and has paid off its mortgage, but
Polly, the star of the show, realizes she misses
Bobby so she leaves for New York to
find him but as she leaves, Bobby runs in and
learns the show he prepared saved the theatre so
he has accomplished something but then
Everett and Mother see each other and fall in love
and sing a duet until Polly reappears and as
Polly and Bobby run into each other's arms and
sing and dance the Finale.

Sitting in the front row, watching the dancers
sweat fly off their faces, we laughed and cried,
applauded and cheered, and lead the house in
a standing ovation. And we don't even like
musicals or Americana that much! That's how
great the show was.

Everybody in the Stratford Festival Theatre
walked out singing songs from the show and
saying it was the best production they had ever
seen, including us, and that was really
saying something huge.

We walked from the Festival Theatre back to
our hotel on Albert Street, called the
Albert Street Inn, past Tim Horton's, which
was closed, and Balzac's, which was also
closed. It looked like all of Stratford was
closed, even though the theatre was just
getting out and people were looking for
places to go, to get a snack and yak about
the play they just saw. But Balzac's was
closed, so we talked about the play all the way
home and then hit the sack.

I know what you're thinking, or wondering,
or assuming, about the two of us
hitting the sack together, but
get your mind out of the gutter,
man, we're just friends. I told Cyn
"I'm crazy for you" and she just said,
"I know" and that's as far as we go.

We laughed hard and long at the
jokes in the musical aimed at
romantic love and marriage and
the whole house roared when
Bobby and Polly were arguing like
an old married couple and he
made a joke about it, saying
We may as well be married, already,
and it got a huge laugh from
the Festival Theatre crowd
if not from us.

As we walked by Balzac's
Cyn said, Do you think
Balzac would have
liked that play? So
I said, I dunno, I don't
think American musicals
would turn his crank;
King Lear might be
more his kind of thing.
Balzac is sometimes called
the Shakespeare of France
but more often he's called
France's Dickens.

The Dickens, you say,
Cyn said, as we parted
for the evening, and I quoted
Shakespeare, saying it was
such sweet sorrow.

Crazy For Stratford

The morning after
Crazy For You
we had breakfast at Balzac's
with coffee again and I stayed to
write while Cyn ran off to
get her nails done and while
I was writing, inspired by
Balzac, one more time,
one of the stars of
Crazy For You
walked in, ordered
coffee, and walked out
again, just like that, as though
she was a mere mortal and
not a big star of the big
musical hit at the
Stratford Festival that summer.

On Facebook, I posted an
up-date to my status:
the star of the show, Natalie Daradich,
Polly Baker in the Stratford Festival's
Crazy for You, just walked in to
Balzac's Coffee. luv this place!

A few people "liked" it
right away and Catherine Gillis
a colleague in China, posted
this comment: Torq one day,
a star the next, that place sounds like
they must serve EPIC coffee!

Torq was a four-piece percussion group
that did a pop-up performance at
Balzac's while we had breakfast
and they did a big show on
Tom Percussion Island in the
Avon River the night before,
with fireworks, which

reminded me of China,
of course, where we have
fireworks every day, and
an incredible fireworks display
on the big holidays, and I
made a one minute video of
the group as they did an
impromptu experimental
jazzy piece after picking up
old coffee cans from a
display in Balzac's and
using them as their
musical instruments and
announcing that it would be
the first and last time
anyone heard it and they
called it Balzac's Blend,
naming it after one of the
coffees you can buy at
Balzac's, but I got it on
video, using my iPhone,
and posted it on Facebook,
so everybody could see it
and hear it as many times
as they wanted, and
I thought it was great.

Cyn and I were both wearing our
Toronto Novel Marathon tee-shirts
and I gave a ToNoMa button to
the woman who travelled with
the four guys in the band as their
producer or whatever and
after the band did a couple of
jazzy percussion numbers
we called for an encore and
that was when they grabbed
the ancient coffee cans and
turned them into jazzy new
musical instruments for
a tune they improvised

on the spot but sounded
like first draft perfect poetry
or a first draft perfect
novella created at a
marathon, inspired by the
energy of group of creative
writers inspired by
each other and it inspired
me to write more jazzy poetry
Shakespeare's King Lear

You probably studied King Lear in
high school, if you are a certain age
and went to Grade Thirteen in
Ontario or took a Shakespeare course
in university or if you are a
teacher and did the AQ course
at the Stratford Campus of the
U of T, or UT/OISE, like me, so
you know the play is all about
an aging monarch who resolves to
divide his kingdom among his
three daughters, with consequences
he little expects.
His reason is shattered in
the storm of violent emotion
that ensues, with his very
life hanging in the balance,
and Lear loses everything that has
defined him as a king – and discovers
the essence of his own humanity.

Cyn said, The reviews are great, and
she read me a few:
"If you have been longing to encounter
greatness in the theatre, it's waiting for you at
the Stratford Festival" – Toronto Star

"unquestionably catapults Colm Feore into
the ranks of the world's greatest living actors"
– Toronto Star

"powerful" – The Globe and Mail "unforgettable"
"a production that will most assuredly not be surpassed
this season–or any season soon." – Kitchener Record
"amazing" - Detroit Free Press -" brilliant"
"the performance of the season at Stratford"
- Hamilton Spectator - "a masterful, powerful performance"
and "epic" according to the Pittsburgh Post-Gazette
We went to the evening performance, our second day
in Stratford, and sat up high, in the first row of the
balcony, and a big guy who looked like Balzac sat
right beside me so he could snore and fart through
the first half of the 2014 Stratford production of
King Lear starring Colm Feore. Before the play started
Balzac's double asked me a question about the play:
Is that Colm Farrari guy the same guy that was in
the new Spiderman movie? And what could I do
except nod mutely while having a Walter Mitty moment
imagining Balzac's twin getting pushed over the
balcony and landing on the seats down below
dying too quickly and not quite painfully enough

At the interval, Cyn said, Did Shakespeare have
his heart broken by a loved one suffering from
a deteriorating mind?
I didn't answer as it was not that kind of a question
and I knew what she was referring to as her
mother just celebrated her 93rd birthday and
Cyn is writing a book about the experience called
Losing Hold of Helen, coming soon to a book store near
you, we hope. And what can I say except
there are moments in King Lear, particularly in
the Stratford Festival's new production of the play
starring Colm Feore, from Spiderman, that will
ring absolutely real to anyone who has watched
an ageing relative losing his or her mind to dementia.

The most powerful moment comes when Cordelia
played by Sara Farb, returned from her banishment
and at the bedside of Lear, asks "Sir, you know who I am?"
and he doesn't and he does – and here's the deep,
deep sadness that comes from a father's inability to see his

own daughter, followed by an elation that comes from his
subsequent remembering, all the more sweet because
it may just be fleeting and the scene is more wrenching than
the later, more famous one, when Lear, his dead daughter now
in his arms, enters howling, because the earlier moment is
one of recognition, that prerequisite for tragedy, and
a moment of seeing what is true not just for Lear but
for the audience, or any audience member who has been in
a similar situation – which in our ageing society is almost everyone.

It is hard to say we loved the play and we did not
want to compare it to the musical we saw
the night before but it is safe to say we certainly
appreciated Colm Feore's King Lear but
it left us feeling the opposite way as the play
with all the singing and dancing called
Crazy For You. Or, as Cyn said, I'm not
crazy for Lear.

Toronto Blues

After leaving King Lear a little early,
at the interval, actually, we went
back to the hotel to do crossword
puzzles, one of our favourite things
to do in the evening, and watch a
little TV, one of Cyn's favourite things
to do, although I rarely, almost never,
turn on the TV, since I used to teach
Media, and it ruined the medium
for me, and I was amazed to see
new shows shot in Toronto on
television and Toronto wasn't just
standing in for some city in the
U.S.A., Toronto was playing the part of
Toronto the way Paris plays Paris in
Balzac's books so there were shots of
famous landmarks like the CN Tower
and the avant-garde building of the
Ontario College of Art by the
Art Gallery of Ontario and they
mentioned famous Toronto
street names, like Yonge and
King and it was a lot of fun for me
to see the city I know so well on
the small screen after so many
years of seeing nothing but the
U.S.A. on TV and we had a
good time watching a newish
show called Rookie Blues about
new cops in the big bad city and
Cyn said there was another show
shot in Toronto and set in Toronto
that was something like it and
there were lots of shows like that
on TV now with cops or the FBI
or forensic teams working with
the cops or the FBI and I told her
I used to like watching 24 starring
Keifer Sutherland, son of

Donald Sutherland, who played
Norman Bethune in the big movie
about his life story and she told me
24 was on the air again with a new
season of shows and Donald
Sutherland was a big star again
thanks to the role he played in the
new movie versions of the
Hunger Games trilogy so I had to
thank her for helping me get
caught up on popular culture
as I had spent the past year in
China not watching TV and the
previous decade and a half
not watching TV in Canada
while I was writing hundreds of
books, competing with Balzac,
and beating him, and then
trying to lap him, writing
twice as many books as
the big guy, beating the
Dickens out of him, as
Cyn might say.

Rookie Blues, set in Toronto,
reminded me of Hill Street Blues,
set in New York City, years ago,
so I thought of it as Toronto
Blues, which made me think of
the new hockey team up north
in Bracebridge, the Junior A team,
called the Bracebridge Blues,
taking over from the Bracebridge
Phantoms, a strange name for a
hockey team, where I played against
the Bracebridge Bears for many
years, and you might think I was
getting homesick for Muskoka or
nostalgic about Toronto with a
bad case of the Toronto Blues but
Cyn was always telling me it sounded

like I was homesick for China because
I kept talking about life in China and
about how China should copy
Stratford and make a theatre district
in Dalian, the city of six million, where
I live and work, complete with a
Shakespeare Festival with a lot of
Shakespeare plus some other famous
writers from the West, old and new,
including some Canadians, and
they would want to add some
Chinese plays to their list, of course,
but Cyn kept saying, You should be
where your feet are, live in the
moment, stay in the here and now,
and that's always good advice but
sometimes it's hard to do when
you live on the other side of the
planet and you're not used to
flying around the world to
go to work or for any other reason
and when I check my e-mail or
Facebook there's always
a few messages from my new
crew in China with Haley in
Outer Mongolia and Catherine
telling me to travel around
China and some of the gang
now in Canada with
Golda traveling across the
country and just missing the big
wildfires in the Rockies that
wrecked the air quality in
Edmonton and came way too close
to the beautiful mountain town
called Banff, named after
Banff in Scotland, and of course
the Rocky Mountains of Canada
made me think about the
Yellow Mountains of China and
the Black Mountains by the

Yellow Sea, where I live, and
I got an e-mail from my favourite
doctor, Sophia Wang, who wrote to say
she was happy I was having a good time
in Canada and she was having fun in
JinShiTan as she went to the beach with
her family, three generations, and went
swimming in the Yellow Sea, so
it must have warmed up considerably
after a month of summer days at
around thirty degrees. But this book is
not about China, it's about Stratford,
my favourite town in Canada, or
right up there with Banff and Muskoka,
although Muskoka isn't a town, it's
three towns, and I'm crazy about
them all but Cyn reminds me to
be where my feet are so let's focus on
the fact I'm crazy for you, Stratford,
Crazy For You.
The Cliff-Hanger Ending

Here endeth our play, as
Shakespeare might say
at the end of A Midsummer
Night's Dream, even though
I've only told you about the
first two plays we saw
this summer in Stratford,
Crazy For You and then
King Lear, which we were
not so crazy about, after
loving the American musical,
and we still have A
Midsummer Night's Dream
and Alice Through The
Looking Glass ahead of us,
and the trip back to Toronto,
which would make a
logical conclusion to this
tale, this long poem about

Stratford in the summertime,
but, well, as you know, I'm
working on a two hundred book
sequence so I'm going to
love you and leave you,
as they say, so I can
finish this book and move on to
the next one, which will be a
sequel, so think of this one as
a stand-alone or a prequel,
as I tend to think in
duologies, after a year in
China, the land of yin and
yang, rather than
trilogies, as we do in
Christian countries, but
that's another story, for
another day, as they say,
and I'm going to end this story
the way we end parties in
China -- abruptly, suddenly
announcing it's over, so
everybody gets up to go
at the same time and there's no
denouement or hangers-on or
stragglers at the party, usually
drunk and looking for a
fight, like Hemingway in
Paris After Midnight ....
So, goodbye, farewell, so long,
adieu to you and you and you,
and I'll see you in the next book,
after we see A Midsummer
Night's Dream in Stratford.

A Midsummer Night's Dream In Stratford:
A Very Long Poem

Martin Avery

Audience Advisory: In general, we recommend this production for ages 8 and up, though it does contain occasional elements of sexual humour that some parents may consider unsuitable. The staging employs haze, smoke, ultraviolet light and simulated laser effects. (From the Stratford Festival website for A Midsummer Night's Dream, 2014.)

A Stratford Romance

I lost a novel I wrote a decade or so ago
called A Stratford Romance, all about a
romantic summer in Stratford, and
that happens, sometimes, if you
write a lot of books, so you don't even
remember writing some of them,
which sounds unlikely or even
impossible if you've never
written a book or only written one
or two and I don't remember many of
the details about A Stratford Romance
except for one scene that takes place
on the Festival Theatre Stage at the end of
A Midsummer Night's Dream, and this
sounds like fiction but I swear it
really happened one summer
I spent in Stratford, taking a Drama course,
with a great group of teachers, and we saw
all the productions at Stratford that summer
including The Tempest, Dracula.
A Midsummer Night's Dream
Pride and Prejudice, The Alchemist
The School for Scandal, West Side Story
Macbeth, Glenn, Richard II, and we all
went to see Dream together, so we all
saw the same thing: a lot of slapstick with
the four young lovers played by
Melinda Deines as Hermia, Michelle Giroux as
Helena, Graham Abbey as Lysander and Martin
Albert as Demetrius with Jordan Pettle as
Nick Bottom and Brian Bedford as Puck
plus Seana McKenna as Titania,
Juan Chioran as Oberon, Diane D'Aquila as
Hippolyta, and some fairies, and, more
importantly, we watched when a doctor
got called out of the audience, from his
seat in the front row, and how his date
got called onto the stage, after the play was

over, and she refused to go, at first, but
eventually got talked into it, and when she
got up there, they showed her one of the
special effects, re-creating the moment when
rose petals fall from the sky, or the ceiling,
and just then her date re-appeared, entering
the stage from back-stage, carrying a
cushion, which he tossed on the ground
and then kneeled on, with one knee, as he
got down on one knee to propose to her,
holding up an engagement ring, and
everybody sighed as it was such a
romantic gesture but then gasped because
instead of accepting and giving the guy
a great big kiss his girlfriend slapped his
face and stomped off! And the gossip
we heard the next day was that she was
angry, humiliated, disappointed, ticked
off, because she was a very private person
and believed her engagement should be a
private event, not a showcase with a big
audience, and she decided that the guy
did not know her, if he thought she would
like all that attention, so she decided
marriage to him would be some kind of
over-produced nightmare she would never
like, so she broke it off and took off and
the most romantic proposal we had ever
witnessed turned out to be a complete
bust, a bomb, a performance that got
a very bad review!

I remember that production of Midsummer
as a very romantic retelling of the
well-known story and I remember that
summer as a very romantic time and
I remember that drama course as one of
the best educational experiences and
I have often wondered about that
proposal on the stage after A Midsummer
Night's Dream, how that guy arranged

it all, faking a call for an emergency, so
he got called out of the performance,
the only time I've ever seen that
at Stratford, and how he arranged to
have some of the cast remain on stage
after a standing ovation and curtain calls
and how he got some of the crew to
cooperate as well so they got his
girlfriend to go on stage and showered her
with rose petals, and how it was that he was
so romantic and so wrong, how it was that
he wanted her so much, wanted to marry her
so bad, and how he misjudged the whole
situation so completely. It was a moment
I haven't forgotten, it was so
Shakespearean, such a combination of
romance, comedy, and tragedy, with a body
left bleeding on the stage at the end of the
performance piece.

About Midsummer

Threatened with death if she marries against
her father's wishes, Hermia elopes with her lover,
Lysander, pursued by rival suitor Demetrius and
his spurned admirer, Helena. In the enchanted woods,
love's lunacy reaches its giddiest heights – both for
the bewildered couples and for an aspiring
actor transformed into the unlikely consort of
a fairy queen.

The reviews for the 2014 production of A
Midsummer Night's Dream in Stratford were
pretty impressive, mostly ....

"wonderfully creative" - Sun Media
"hysterical" - Sun Media
"sheer joy" - Sun Media
"palpable sizzle" - The Globe and Mail
"This is a Dream to beguile everyone,
from preteens to the most jaded theatregoers." - The Grid
"... the perfect family celebration of diversity"- The Grid
"****" (out of four) - Detroit Free Press
"among the funniest I have ever seen" - Detroit Free Press
"I can't recall ever seeing a production in which the audience and the actors were having a better time" - Detroit Free Press
"Shakespeare would approve" - Detroit Free Press

However, the Toronto Star's review of
the play was not good. Here's what the
Star had to say, in the form of a poem,
let's call it a found poem, found in the
Toronto Star, or on their website, at
www.thestar.com/cntertainment/stage/
2014/06/01/a_midsummer_nights_dream
A Midsummer Night's Dream: Review
By: Richard Ouzounian Theatre Critic,
Published on Sun Jun 01 2014
A Midsummer Night's Dream
.5 star
By William Shakespeare. Directed by Chris Abraham.

STRATFORD—During the previews of
Chris Abraham's production of
A Midsummer Night's Dream, the word on the street was
that it was a show people would either love or hate.
It opened at the Festival Theatre on Saturday night and
I was there.
Count me among the haters.
Let me make it clear that my dislike of the show
had nothing to do with its central framing device
(that it's all being performed to celebrate the marriage of
two men) or its selective use of gender-blind casting
(Titania is played by a man, Lysander by a woman).
No, what bothered me so profoundly was that it's
the kind of show that will sacrifice any sort of logic for
a cheap laugh and that most of the yocks generated during
the evening come from extraneous business
and cheap anachronistic ad libs, almost never from
the words of William Shakespeare.
Would you like some examples?
If we are indeed in 2014 and are supposed to believe
Hermia and Lysander as a lesbian couple who are
running off together, why would Hermia suddenly
play all coy when they bed down for the night and
hide inside an inflatable tent, which then proceeds to lurch
"humourously" all over the place as
Lysander unsuccessfully puts the moves on her.
And if Lysander then goes to sleep totally wrapped up in
a sleeping bag with no clothes showing, how does
Puck know to sprinkle the love-inducing herb on
her because "Weeds of Athens he doth wear"?
In a later scene, when the same poor lovers suddenly discover
a table full of wedding cake and cupcakes at centre stage
(meant for the wedding celebration), why
do these characters in a play start using the desserts from
the evening's "reality" to generate a massive food fight?
Those are just a few of dozens of examples I could have given.
Director Abraham only cares about how many in-jokes and
wannabe-hipster-meta laughs he can get by mocking the text.
The only person who actually gets away with it is
Mike Shara's Demetrius, who is the frat boy of your nightmares,
but plays it with such dedication and swaggering charm that

you somehow forgive him.
As for the other lovers, Bethany Jillard's Hermia is fine when
she's not whining, Liisa Repo-Martell as Helena seems to have
lost all the subtlety and variety she displayed in King Lear and
Tara Rosling initially makes a fine and sexy Lysander until
she is forced into horrible overdrive by Abraham.
For the rest? Well, Scott Wentworth dispenses his usual
ease on stage and grace with blank verse as Theseus, but
Maev Beaty delivers the first embarrassing performance
I've ever seen out of her as Hippolyta, because
Abraham makes her spend the whole final scene getting
Lindsay Lohan drunk.
As the other "regal" couple, Jonathan Goad has
a nice swagger as Oberon and delivers the poetry with
real edge, but he eventually gets defeated by
the silliness. (There's a pool of water on stage that
it seems everyone has to get drenched in eventually, like
Abraham was running a wet t-shirt contest for the entire cast.)
Evan Buliung as his consort, Titania makes, well, a very
solid woman, but he does a really nice job with his line in
sassy ad libs, even if some of them eventually undercut
the sincerity of Oberon's reconciliation with him.
(For the record, Goad and Buliung alternate the roles,
but I don't think that flip-flop would substantially change the show.)
There are far too many cute kids playing fairies and also
supposedly being adorable singing pop songs, as if
Stratford needed to find another Justin Bieber.
And as the leader of all the fairies, Chick Reid plays
Puck as Judge Judy.
That surely is not the way to do it.
Do those lovable comic characters the rustic mechanicals save
the day? Alas, no.
Stephen Ouimette starts out funny with a conception of Bottom as
a greasy pseudo-macho barbecue king, but
it eventually degenerates into a blandly generic performance.
And the rest of his cohorts have nothing to do with
the rest of the style of the play, with
a final sure-fire comedy scene that
misfires totally for the first time in my memory.
This production has nothing to do with
gender equality, shifting sexual roles or

anything of any real significance.
It's Value Village Shakespeare, a total surprise
coming from Abraham after last year's excellent Othello.
Let's hope this is just an aberration, the kind
that can happen to even a talented director on
a midsummer night.

That's the end of that review.
And what can we say?
Ouch!
My review would not go that way!
Neither did the review in
The Globe And Mail.
Let's give the Globe review
equal time and the same
treatment: This is a found poem,
found in The Globe And Mail online.

A Midsummer Night's Dream:
Stratford gloriously uplifts
overdone Shakespeare comedy
J. Kelly Nestruck
Stratford, Ont. — The Globe and Mail
Published Monday, Jun. 02 2014, 4:20 PM EDT
    Title A Midsummer Night's Dream
    Written by William Shakespeare
    Directed by Chris Abraham
    Starring Stephen Ouimette, Evan Buliung
    Company Stratford Festival

Get into your car, get out to this Dream. Or,
if you live farther than driving distance from
Stratford, Ont., maybe get into a plane or onto a train.
Forgive the bastardized Billy Ocean. I'm just
trying to get into the topsy-turvy, 1980s synth-pop vibe that
animates director Chris Abraham's gloriously uplifting and
revivifying production of
the most overdone of Shakespeare's comedies.
I thought I could live without ever seeing another
A Midsummer Night's Dream.
But how can you not love a version that features

the comic genius Stephen Ouimette as Bottom
barbecuing in a "Daddio of the Patio" apron
at the beginning, then singing New Order's
Bizarre Love Triangle amid a raging dance party at the end?
(Consider that a warning, too: If you can't, then you won't.)

Bottom, of course, is the weaver and amateur actor transformed
into a donkey who stars in the play-within-a-play that concludes
A Midsummer Night's Dream. His awful production of
Pyramus and Thisbe is presented as a gift at the nuptials of
Athenian rulers Theseus and Hippolyta, as well as
those of the play's quartet of lovers, finally and properly matched.

In Abraham's vision of the show, however, the entirety of
Dream is presented as a wedding gift – to two young men
getting married in a Stratford, Ont., backyard. Thus,
this Dream is presented with a host of young children
(who play the fairies, not just cutely, but astutely, and
never fail to bring a smile to your face) in the cast, an
onstage wedding DJ providing synth underscoring and
sound effects throughout, and the cream of the crop of
Stratford's acting company essaying unexpected roles and
treating the show and their parts with the irreverent joy and
anachronistic fun that you might in such a situation.

In a play that is about love and transformation,
Abraham has, fittingly, made a few changes to the characters.
At the start of the play, Hermia (Bethany Jillard) wants to
marry Lysander (Tara Rosling), but
her father Egeus wants her to marry Demetrius
(preening Mike Shara);
on the outside looking in is Helena (Liisa Repo-Martell),
who wants her ex Demetrius back.
The twist here is that Lysander is played as a woman by
a woman – and Rosling displays great nobility pleading her
love in the role at the start. "I am beloved of beauteous Hermia:
Why should not I then prosecute my right?"
she says movingly, and with same-sex rights denied in
so much of the world still, this acquires a
powerful resonance that it usually does not
(but which is probably roughly equivalent to

the resonance the original situation had in Shakespeare's time).

The other major shift is that Jonathan Goad and Evan Buliung play
the monarchs of the fairy world, Oberon and Titania, and
alternate between the roles.
On opening night, Buliung was the Fairy Queen –
and, despite his cis-male status, he was the best
I have ever seen,
regal and eerily otherworldly
(and never for a moment like a panto dame).
He and Goad, who
takes great advantage of the production's concept to
ad lib and play to the audience, have a
palpable sizzle in a part of the play that really feels like
it takes place in another dimension.
(Thank composer/sound designer Thomas Ryder Payne,
who also plays the DJ, in part for this.)

Shakespeare at Stratford is not particularly known for
sexual chemistry – but Jillard and Rosling have it
in spades here too, especially in a cleverly staged and
very hot scene that takes place away from
the audience's eyes inside of a camping tent set up
on stage. Abraham allow endless opportunities for
well-executed physical comedy here –
Rosling pulls some fine Pepé le Pew moves when
Lysander is under the influence of Puck's love juice, while
Shara gets many of the best moments preening as
Demetrius, rotating slowly in Helena's imagination, or
throwing children-fairies across the stage in a fury.

The Mechanicals, which include Lally Cadeau as
an uptight Peter Quince, are not perhaps
the funniest I've seen – but, for once,
their scenes seem in balance with the rest of the play.
And, thanks to Abraham's framing of the evening,
I finally really understood why Shakespeare includes
their performance of the tragedy of Pyramus and Thisbe
at the end. These wise fools are showing
what happens when you erect ridiculous walls
(and Keith Dinicol is an especially ridiculous Wall here)

between love;
it's that world, the one of tragedy, that is foolish,
while the world Bottom describes –
where "reason and love keep little company together"
– is the happy and sensible one.

There are moments one could quibble with:
Chick Reid's Puck and Liisa Repo-Martell's Helena are
remarkably unremarkable in parts that are usually
fan favourites, while the whole quartet of lovers occasionally
blast their verse into oblivion amid the mayhem.
Abraham's production also ends in what seems like
an endless competition of epilogues between
Bottom, Oberon, Puck and Theseus –
and it's a shame that though Egeus is played as
deaf in the play,
a deaf actor wasn't hired for this rare opportunity
to play at Stratford.

But this is a production better to just love blindly.
"There's no sense in telling me the wisdom of the fool won't
set you free," sings Bottom, who, by the end of the play,
knows a thing or two about bizarre love triangles.
And, yes, beyond the laughs and a few joyful tears, there is
something about Abraham's Dream that makes you feel
as if you've been set free, particularly after
an opening week of solid, but stuffy versions of
classic plays at Stratford.

Follow J. Kelly Nestruck on Twitter: @nestruck
More Related to this Story
Crazy for You: Stellar choruses plus
thrilling choreography equals
an exhilarating musical

Shakespeare And Cleopatra

Before we saw the Stratford 2014 production
of A Midsummer Night's Dream, we
wandered through the Festival store across
from the Theatre to browse books and
recordings and tee-shirts and other souvenirs
of the Stratford Festival Theatre for the
summer and discovered funky dolls for
Cleopatra and Shakespeare sitting side by
side on matching tables against a wall so
I picked up one of each and made them
trade places so Shakespeare was surrounded
by Cleopatras and Cleo was surrounded by
Shakespeares and picked up a pair to show
Cyn who surprised me after I said that
a lot of people who do past life work say
they were somebody famous and a lot of
women claim they were Cleopatra but
only a few men say they were Shakespeare
and she said, That was us, but I was
Shakespeare and you were Cleopatra.
She has an odd way of talking, sometimes,
so it sounds she is quite certain about
some things, speaking with the voice of
authority, and it sounded as though she
knew in her bones that she was a man
in a previous lifetime and that man was
William Shakespeare and I was quite
surprised by that but even more surprised
the she was quite certain I was a famous
woman from Egypt who happens to be
someone I quote quite often, as I like to say,
"Endless variety," and claim it comes from
Cleopatra and I often think about past lives,
unlike Cyn, and past lives in Egypt, and
time travel using Egypt as a portal or
station and I've written about the pyramids
when they were covered with an
encyclopedia of information which
they say Jesus studied and I've dreamed

about having a past life in Alexandria or
Cairo or somewhere along the Nile that
looks like the Garden of Eden when
time travel was common and popular and
I was a time travel agent arranging trips
from one time and place to another and
2. Back At Balzac's For Breakfast Again

Cyn and I spent the morning, lunch, and
afternoon at Balzac's again, from around
11 in the morning, after breakfast at our
hotel, the St. Albert Inn, or their
restaurant, called Let Them Eat Cake,
until around 4 in the afternoon, over
five hours, drinking strong coffee and
writing like Balzac, surrounded by
Balzac posters, inhaling Balzac Blend
coffee, watching Fiona Reid walk in and
out again, like a character in
The Time Traveller's Wife and
Cyn was working on her book, her
memoir, her autobiography, called
God Shots, which I wanted her to call
Hollywood, Hell, And Home, while
I finished book one in this duology
and changed the title from
Breakfast With Balzac, Lunch With Fellini
to Crazy For Stratford, and published it
online through Lulu and then started
right in on book #2 of the two, which
doesn't have a title yet, maybe
I'll call the two books together
Breakfast With Balzac, Lunch With Fellini
or The Yin And Yang Of Stratford or
maybe another title will pop into my head
as I write this long poem.

How I love long poems, now; they are
new to me but as old as literature, older
than Shakespeare, and perfect for me at
this stage as they all for all the freedom of

freefall or free-writing in free verse which
allows me to go at the speed I feel like
writing these days which is one hundred
miles per hour as I am jacked up on
Balzac's cafe mocha and Cyn likes to
see me speeding on Red Bull and
I've spent the last year in China getting
Traditional Chinese Medicine including
fire cupping with tu-nai or finger needling
with acupuncture including warm needles
and don't forget moxibustion and herbal
patches as well as tea and a formula to
drink so my chi or energy is flowing like
never before or not since I was a
young punk, a long time ago, now, but
it doesn't feel like it, and I'm writing
faster and better than ever, I believe, after
writing 100 books in The West and then
moving to The East to write 100 more, and
it took me decades to write the first thirty
and under a year to write the last thirty so
here we go with #140 (or so).

Our Review Of Midsummer Night

We really liked the 2014 production of
A Midsummer Night's Dream in
Stratford from the moment we walked in
to the moment we walked out. While we
waited for the play to start, we watched
the seats fill up with audience members and
we noticed that they all looked older than
us, with a few exceptions, and they all looked
as though they had spent their whole lives
reading books and watching plays, or
movies, not jogging or swimming, so
they looked like intellectuals, not athletes.
What did you expect? Cyn said. This is a
theatre, not a gym. We liked
the Festival Theatre stage, decorated to
look like a back yard in Muskoka, we
decided, with a lot of green, including
grass and trees, with a little pond, plus
patio lanterns, and it reminded me of
Cyn's back yard. If only it had a guy
practicing guitar on the back door steps,
I said, because her big brother used to
do that all the time, and then a guy
came out to play guitar, and then
the play started with two guys kissing
at centre stage, a white man and a
black man, and we knew we were in for
a night of theatre that would challenge
contemporary ideas about relationships
in a way Shakespeare would not have
done it but in a way that might be on the
same level as the way he did it back in
his day. I'd rather see a traditional or
classic production of this play, Cyn said,
at the interval, or half-time, when we
went for a walk, to stretch our legs,
and kept on walking, all the way back
to our little hotel, just ten blocks or so
away from the theatre, and we felt a

little bad about missing the second half
but the reviews suggested it turned into
a wet tee-shirt contest and we were
a little tired after seeing three plays in
three days with one more the next day
so we didn't feel too bad about missing
half of Midsummer, even though we
missed half of King Lear, the day before,
and it was a much more traditional
production, more like Shakespeare
would have done it, although the
emphasis was not on the plot, it was on
the star, it was all about King Lear, as
an aging ruler suffering from dementia
and we both had people close to us who
were suffering from dementia, so,
you know how it goes, sometimes,
when a play or movie strikes a little too
close to home and you can appreciate
the artistry and even benefit from the
catharsis of seeing a situation that's
important to you on the stage with
great actors but it's just not what you
want to see at the moment, and so
we did not stay for the second half of
either of the Shakespearean productions
at Stratford in the summer of 2014 and
that's not meant as a judgement on the
plays or actors or any aspect of the
experience, it was just what we wanted
to do at the time, and we felt free to
do what we wanted to do, and we were
happy we did it, despite the fact we
wanted to experience and celebrate
everything the Stratford Festival
had to offer. It was like skipping dessert
after a fantastic meal: we didn't
need it or want it even though we
recognized the fact that it would
be terrific.

Prolific Authors

Good news and bad news tonight
from around the world and
right here at home. First of all,
a Malaysian Airlines plane was
shot down over Ukraine and
hundreds died.
A Boeing 777 passenger plane of
the Malaysia Airlines crashed in
eastern Ukraine en route from
Amsterdam to Kuala Lumpur with
all 295 people on board feared dead.
The Ukrainian government and
rebels in the region accused each other
of shooting down the plane.
Secondly, wildfires out west in Canada are
the biggest in history, apparently,
and are threatening the town of
Banff as well as polluting the
skies of Edmonton.

Here in Stratford, my car got
stickered for being parked in the wrong
place. And then I Googled the
list of the world's most
prolific authors and discovered
I do not have a shot at the
record. The good news is that
I might be able to break into
the top twenty. The other news is
that I no longer care, because of
the other news from Malaysia
and Ukraine and Western Canada.

In case you care, here's the list
of the most prolific authors in
the history of the planet:

1. MARY FAULKNER (1903-1973) 904 books
South African writer Mrs. Mary Faulkner, whom

the Guinness Book of World Records ranks as
history's most prolific novelist, wrote under
six pen names and her novels include
There Is No Yesterday, Wind of Desire, and Harvest of Deceit.

2. LAURAN PAINE (b. 1916) 850 + books
American paperback novelist using 70 pen names.
Paine wrote a lot of westerns, such as
The Man from Wells Fargo (1961).

3. PRENTISS INGRAHAM (1843-1904) 600 + books
American dime novelist who occasionally wrote a
35,000-word book overnight. He wrote 200 books on Buffalo Bill alone.

9. GEORGES SIMENON (b. 1903) 500 + books
Belgian-born mystery writer with more than 200 books
published under his own name and over 300 published
under 17 pen names. His most famous character is Inspector Maigret.

11. EDWARD L. STRATEMEYER (1862-1930) 400 + books
American founder of the publishing syndicate that put out
the Nancy Drew and Hardy Boys and other popular children's series.

19. ALEXANDRE DUMAS pere (1802-1870) 277 books
The famous French author of The Three Musketeers and
The Count of Monte Cristo said to Napoleon III that he had
written 1,200 volumes, but that, of course, was in the days of
multivolume novels. (Musketeers originally filled eight volumes.)
His complete works were collected in 277 volumes,
most of which he wrote with collaborators.

20. L. T. MEADE (1854-1914) 258 books

It was a strange day for Cyn and I as we
wrote for over five hours in Balzac's and then
we were cranky so we went our
separate ways for the rest of the afternoon and
the early evening but got together again for
A Midsummer's Night Dream at the
Stratford Festival Theatre and we liked the
production but left at the interval because

we were tired and then I discovered
my car got stickered and the world news was
depressing, the national news was worse, and
the most prolific writers in the history of
literature have written ten times as many
books as me.

Cyn and I decided to call it a night early
but I stayed up to 11 surfing the net and
working on this book, but then I
hit the sack, hoping to
meditate my way to sleep while
remembering to work on
enlightenment so the evening would end
on a higher note and the next day would be
better than this one.

Southern Ontario Gothic

Friday morning, after an unsettled day,
I got up early to feed the meter, make sure
the car was okay, and decided to keep our
rooms for another day, so we would be
free to come and go as we pleased.
Cyn slept in so I had the breakfast special at
Let Them Eat Cake by the Albert Street Inn
on my own, feeling lonely, missing my
old life in China, feeling reverse
culture shock after seventeen days in my
home and native land.
I have bags under my eyes the likes of which
I've never had before and I feel a little tired,
which is odd, for me, so maybe international
travel does not agree with me. I've never
been a jet-setter so traveling half way around
the world and back is new to me and maybe
it's tiring me out. I'm saying "maybe"
a lot and I guess that means I'm not feeling
certain about .... anything.
Is that part of culture shock, or reverse
culture shock? What is it I miss about
China, or Asia, or is it just Dalian, my
little corner of the big continent and
the crowded country, the city of
six million called the Paris of China.
I've been writing about Balzac and
feeling his presence a great deal and
Balzac wrote about Paris and now
I live in the Paris of China and
think of myself as the Balzac of
China, in a way, as well as the
Balzac of Canada. Oy veh! That's not
the way I think of myself at all!
I'm just a guy who writes a lot and
teaches high school and likes
books and theatre and nature and
worries about the planet's politics
and environment. I feel worried

this morning, which is not usual
for me. Maybe I need more sleep.
Maybe I need more love. Maybe
I miss the excitement of my
life in China and all the love
I felt while I was there. I miss
seeing so many Asian faces,
being the only white face in
a big crowd, feel funny sitting in
the audience of the Stratford Festival
theatre surrounded by white people
who are not thin and look as though
they have spent their lives
sitting around reading books and
watching plays and movies and
not running around trying to
survive the way the people of
Dalian have for the past
half century, or longer. I thought
Canadians were a long stronger.
Maybe the white faces I see
around me belong to Americans
who have crossed the border,
leaving the U.S.A. for Canada
in the summer, to see
Shakespeare in Stratford.
Maybe, maybe, maybe.

I woke up thinking about
Timothy Findlay: Timothy Irving
Frederick Findley, OC, O.Ont.,
 a Canadian novelist and playwright,
informally known by the nickname
Tiff or Tiffy, an acronym of his initials.
I saw his star on the sidewalk by the
Avon Theatre while I was walking
yesterday, looking for Red Bull and
Preparation H. -- Too much information?
I was looking for energy and for
something to take away the
bags under my eyes so I

looked energized and felt
like going to the theatre to see
A Midsummer Night's Dream.

Tiff? Cyn said. Who's that?
She loves Canada but has never
been a huge fan of CanLit
until now. Timothy Findlay
was part of the original
Stratford Festival company in
the 1950s, acting alongside
Alec Guinness, and also played in
Sunshine Sketches,
the CBC Television adaptation of
Stephen Leacock's Sunshine Sketches
of a Little Town.

Findley declared his homosexuality as
a teenager, but married actress/photographer
Janet Reid for a couple of years and
eventually became the domestic partner of
writer Bill Whitehead. They collaborated on
several documentary projects in the 1970s,
including the television miniseries
The National Dream and Dieppe 1942.

Findley's first two novels,
The Last of the Crazy People (1967) and
The Butterfly Plague (1969), were
published in Britain and the United States
after having been rejected by Canadian publishers.
Findley's third novel, The Wars, was
published to great acclaim and went on to win
the Governor General's Award for fiction and
was adapted for film in the 1980s.

Timothy Findley was a founding member
and chair of the Writers' Union of Canada
and a president of the Canadian chapter of
PEN International. His writing was typical of
the Southern Ontario Gothic style —

Findley, in fact, first invented its name —
and was heavily influenced by Jungian psychology.
Mental illness, gender and sexuality were
recurring themes in his work. His characters
carried dark personal secrets, and were
conflicted — sometimes to the point of psychosis.

Findley and Whitehead resided at
Stone Orchard, a farm near Cannington,
Ontario, and in the south of France, and
Findley was honoured by the French,
who declared him a
Chevalier de l'Ordre des arts et des lettres.

Findley was the author of dramas for
television and stage. Elizabeth Rex,
his most successful play, premiered at
the Stratford Festival of Canada to
rave reviews and won him another
Governor General's award.

 In the final years of Findley's life,
declining health led him to move
his Canadian residence to
Stratford, Ontario, and he in 2002, in
Brignoles, France, not far from
his place in Cotignac.

He would have loved Stratford's
2014 production of Midsummer
Night's Dream, I think. I saw his
play here in Stratford, Elizabeth
Rex, and I've read his novels, and
taught The Wars several times.

I feel close to Tiff this morning,
here in Stratford, like a strange
character in a novel in the sytle
of Southern Ontario Gothic.

Cottage Gothic

My first book was called Cottage Gothic
and book stores often placed it in the
architecture or building section of their
stores as the term gothic refers to
architecture and cottage gothic is the
term used to describe

What is Gothic literature?
That which we classify as "Gothic" is a subgenre of
the Romantic movement of the 19th century
starting with Horace Walpole's novel
The Castle of Otranto. -- I like that name,
Otranto .... Sounds like a mash-up of
Ontario and Toronto .... Maybe I'll use it ....

Originally, what we call "Gothic" in terms of architecture
was called the modern or French style by its contemporaries
and Gothic architecture was all about the introduction of
light and height to the churches through the use of
flying buttresses, pointed arches, ribbed vaulting and
stained glass windows. The idea was for the church to
become a medium between Earth and Heaven through
its height and the heavenly light.

Gothic Cottage may refer to Carpenter Gothic,
the architectural style, or Rural Gothic, a
North American architectural style using
wood for details that were carved in stone
in authentic Gothic architecture, characterized by
its profusion of jig-sawn details, after
the invention of the steam-powered scroll saw
often using board and batten siding.

"American Gothic" is a painting by
Grant Wood from 1930 inspired by
a cottage designed in the Carpenter Gothic
style with a distinctive upper window and
a decision to paint the house along with
"the kind of people I fancied should live in that house."

So... what is Gothic literature?
Gothic is a genre that incorporates themes of
eternal conflict and importance to
the human condition - relationships, gender,
patriarchy, nostalgia, and the sublime.
It looks away from the present to the past and
from what is obvious and scientific towards
an inner world that is at once liberating and
imprisoning, and forces the reader to
engage it on its own terms, and not those of
social and cultural conditioning.

For Southern Ontario Gothic, think of
Timothy Findlay and Margaret Atwood and
Alice Munro, who won the Nobel Prize in
Literature, and for Central Ontario Gothic,
which is a little different, think of
Susan Swan and Mel Malton and me, and
for Canadian Gothic, think of Bear by
Marian Engel. -- I've met all these writers
and got to know some of them and I've
worked with others and feel
related to all of them.

When I was in grad school in the U.S.A.,
working with writers from all over America,
it did not surprise me that I hit it off with
Wally Lamb, who had a background
something like mine, but I was shocked
to discover I had a great deal in common
with a group of women writers from the
American South, but then I realized they
were writing American Gothic, or
American South Gothic, and we were all
writing about repression and the longing
for liberation, setting our stories in
moody places, like the Ontario described by
Susanna Moodie in Roughing It In The
Bush and "Life in the Backwoods, A Sequel to
Roughing it in the Bush" and Life in

the Clearings Versus the Bush.
-- Makes me think of my old hometown in
Muskoka called Gravenhurst which means
a graven clearing in a forest, the setting of
around half of my first 100 books.

P.S. I just Googled myself, looking for
Cottage Gothic, and discovered my
first book is now available for free along with
an audio book version, apparently, at
http://bookdir.info/?p=114934, with
a couple of great reviews.

Alice Through the Looking-Glass

By Lewis Carroll
Adapted for the stage by James Reaney
Directed by Jillian Keiley
Approximate running time:
2 hrs 12 min, including one interval

About the Play
Climbing through her living-room mirror,
Alice enters a world of wonders populated by
such fantastical characters as Humpty Dumpty,
Tweedledee and Tweedledum, the Walrus and
the Carpenter – and the fearsome Jabberwock.
Children and adults alike will be delighted by
this spectacular journey into the topsy-turvy
realm of the dreaming mind.

"visual and choreographic feast" - Toronto Star
"kaleidoscope of visual delight for kids of all ages"
"ideal for the whole family" - The Record
"childhood imagination reigns supreme"
"magical" - "great fun" - Sun Media

Audience Advisory
Recommended for ages 6 and up,
this production uses pyrotechnics.

Alice Through the Looking-Glass: Review
A visual and choreographic feast,
Alice Through the Looking-Glass really is
one show that's for kids of all ages.
By: Richard Ouzounian Theatre Critic,
Published on Sat May 31 2014
Alice Through the Looking-Glass

By James Reaney. Directed by
Jillian Keiley at the Avon Theatre.
Call it Cirque du Stratford.
The production of Alice Through the

Looking-Glass at the Avon Theatre
is so filled with visual velocity and
choreographic charm that our
show business cousins up in Quebec
had better look to their laurels.
Either that, or ask Jillian Keiley to
direct and Bretta Gerecke to design
their next production, as they have
done so splendidly with this one.

Let's be honest, the "Family Entertainment" slot
that Stratford has been hawking for some time now
is fraught with terrors. Some shows that
charm the real youngsters bore the teens silly and
perplex the parents, while others
that mom and dad enjoy find
brother and sister swatting each other with
programs before intermission.

But now for something completely different, as
Monty Python would say, and in fact, this totally
bizarre version of Alice Through the Looking-Glass is
like the child that the iconic British comedy troupe
might have conceived if they'd spent a wild night with
Guy Laliberté and his merry Québécois pranksters.

The script is by the late and venerable James Reaney,
based on Lewis Carroll's oft-adapted story of
what happens when a girl named Alice goes through a
looking-glass, down a rabbit hole, or
any combination of the above.

At first, this version starts straight and a bit slowly, but
once Trish Lindström's Alice (slightly off-centre with
a welcome touch of Amy Poehler about her) goes through
the mirror, it's anything goes and the devil take the hindmost.

At times, every member of the large cast, young and old,
male and female are all dressed like photographic negatives of
Alice: dark hair while hers is blond, wearing
blue pinafores dotted with white, whereas

Alice wears white dotted with blue.

That's simple to say, less simple to see, especially
when the drag acts include Tom McCamus,
Sanjay Talwar and Brian Tree, all of whom
make very odd young women indeed.

Then there's the younger men, like
Tyrone Savage or Gareth Potter, who
hold on to their handsome masculinity and
let it shine through the feminine disguise.
It's all strangely provocative.
But most of the time, it's just fun.
And it's spectacular fun as the cast members use
roller skates to move giant metal "trees" covered with
a variety of spectacular objects to take us into
that place truly known as Wonderland.
Just like a golden oldies radio program,
the hits keep a-comin', and I am loath to
give away too many of the surprises that include
cascading jelly beans, confetti cannons and
gigantic foam letters that spell, of course, A-L-I-C-E.
Yes, it's a non-stop riot, thanks to
Keiley's staging (assisted by Dayna Tekatch's eclectic
choreography), but now and then we actually
pause to allow some of the familiar scenes from
Carroll's work to emerge, interpreted with
total panache by the company.
You will be totally entranced by
Cynthia Dale's archly regal Red Queen, sending up
sky-high all the glamour-pusses she's ever played at
Stratford, or Brian Tree's magnificently sour
Humpty Dumpty, sprinkling a fine mist of
malt-vinegar pessimism on the
fish-and-chips comedy of his character.
You won't be able to get enough of
the Tweedledum of Mike Nadajewski,
collapsing on stage repeatedly like a
narcoleptic rag doll, or his partner,
the Tweedledee of Sanjay Talwar, who keeps
running in circles like a dog chasing its tail,

both of them delivering the ooziest
North Country accents you've ever heard.
And mention must, must, must be made of
the one and only Tom McCamus, whose
March Hare has droopy eyes any
basset hound would envy and whose
narrator is briskly wheeled onto the stage in
an armchair for a parody of
Masterpiece Theatre to deliver the richest
version of "Jabberwocky" you've ever heard.
To be totally honest, not every one of the
characterizations works, but those lapses are
few and far between, and the beautiful thing about
Keiley's production is that it's like
Vancouver weather: if you don't like it, wait
five minutes and it will change.
You know that much-abused phrase: for
children of all ages? This smashing production of
Alice Through the Looking-Glass truly deserves it.

If you don't know a child, rent one for
the afternoon and go see this show.

Review: Well played, Stratford, well played.
Alice Through the Looking-Glass at the Avon Theatre
Alice Through the Looking-Glass, by Lewis Carroll
Adapted for the stage by James Reaney
Produced in association with Canada's National Arts Centre
Directed by Jillian Kelley
Choreographed by Dayna Tekatch
Designed by Bretta Gerecke

The Story: Alice, having been sent to
her room "until she learns better manners",
retreats into her imagination, which takes her
into the world of her looking-glass, where
everything happens backwards. As she
makes her way across a giant chessboard to
become a queen, she meets a wide range of
impossible characters doing impossible
things, until she begins to suspect she is in

a dream - but whose dream is it?

Talk about a testament to the craftsmanship of
the props and costumes departments at
the Stratford Festival.
An army of anti-Alices in blue-and-white dresses,
wheeling around on an armada of bicycles attached to
which are a forest of trees (onto which the leaves fall
up) and giant flowers - not to mention the
inevitable mess of Newtonian fluid that is
all that is left of Humpty Dumpty after
he takes his great fall off his great wall.
And let us not forget the mile high or wide
prop-wigs worn by the White and Red Queens that
look like they weigh about ten pounds each.
My neck hurts just thinking about it.

Well, it is a fantasy after all, things are bound to
look quite fantastic, and the story makes about as
much sense as adult rules do to the children
like Alice who are expected to follow them.
Director Jillian Kelley's concept for the
production is as clear as it is likely to get with
such a story, the actors are given free reign to
be as over-the-top as necessary, and
the show often breaks the fourth wall -
to great effect for an audience full of children.

In fact, since the Stratford Festival has
marketed this production of
Alice Through the Looking-Glass for children since
the very start, I thought it only fair to
let my review be written by those for whom it was intended.
So at intermission I asked Ellie, Isaac, Berkeley and Miles
if they were enjoying the show, and why.
Ellie (age 6), wearing a sparkly mask in
the true spirit of the show, answered with
an enthusiastic "Yes! I want to know
what will happen next!" and confessed
she did not like the fire (sparklers, actually),
"because" she explained quite awed,

"I had the funny feeling it was real.
But my favourite part was when she
[Alice] touched the mirror and it went
around and around - it was really cool!"

Miles (age 4) liked a different part.
"Yeah," he said, "I liked when the bikes came out,"
referencing the bikes that became trees,
flowers and other gigantic props, "but
I like it all." (Miles also got to pull a
giant rope in the second half of the show after
intermission which no doubt became
his personal highlight.
I won't spoil what the rope-pulling wrought,
but it was a delightfully sweet surprise.)

Isaac (age 5) had the same favourite character as
the rest - Alice (played by Trish Lindstrom). "But
I really liked when the Red Queen said,
"Goodbye!" and jumped off the stage!"
This was actress Cynthia Dale, literally
throwing herself into the part, which
the young audience definitely appreciated if
Isaac was any indication.
But Berkeley (age 5) felt quite differently.
When asked if she was enjoying the show, she
answered with a grave frown and shake of
the head. Oh dear. "Why not, Berkeley?" I asked.
"It's too confusing," she said, still grave, and
patted her cheek. Her grandmother Gretchen
explained, "she didn't understand the part about
the gnat, and it bothered her" referencing
the talking bug that is both an actor
behind Alice an invisible mite that
Alice keeps swatting at and eventually smites
(by accident). At this point
Berkeley was pulling out a recent purchase from
the gift shop and leafing through it -
a copy of Alice in Wonderland.
"Berkeley, do you think you'll enjoy
the book more than the play?" I asked.

"YES!" came the emphatic reply. Oh dear.

Ok, so we head into the second half of the play,
where the Lion and the Unicorn
(Tyrone Savage and Gareth Potter respectively) have a
boxing / karate / mixed-martial-arts battle, we meet
Humpty Dumpty on his great wall - played to
absolute perfection by Brian Tree with
assistance from two of the anti-Alice Army -
and where the White Knight (Rylan Wilkie)
vanquishes the Red Knight (John Kirkpatrick),
serenades Alice, Alice finally becomes
a queen and returns to her own home.
My personal highlights?
Sarah Orenstein as a delightful White Queen,
bouncing around with that mile-high wig, and
Brian Tree's Humpty Dumpty, incidentally
the only actor whose English accent didn't sound
put on because he is English, and the
blink-and-you'll-miss-it-for-adults-only
Last Supper tableau (cheeky, wot?)

But back to the critics who matter.
I tracked some of them down at shows' end.
Kaelynn (age 4) loved the Red Queen, and
when the White Knight sang to Alice
(a future musical theatre aficionado, methinks).
Her brother Kaine (age 5) loved
Tweedledee and Tweedledum
(Liverpudlian-sounding Sanjay Talwar and
Mike Nadajewski respectively) pulling Alice into
a game of Ring Around the Rosie, and
adamantly did NOT like "the part where
they put her [Alice] in her room." Understandably.

Clare (age 10) thought the whole thing "very cool.
The streamers and jellybeans were unexpected."
(Oh, spoiler alert!) Clare also felt that
Trish Lindstrom "captured a 7 and-a-half-year-old
exactly." Her mom Maureen loved
the cross-dressing Alices, which reminded her of

a Mark Morris ballet. "It just flips things
in your brain so you see things in a new way,"
she explained. "It challenges
preconceived ideas. I really enjoyed it."

And at this point Berkeley (age 5), our harshest
critic, came running up. "I really liked the second part!"
she burst out. "Humpty Dumpty was funny."
Her grandmother Gretchen chimed in.
"She perked up a lot with the jellybeans," she chuckled.

Well played, Stratford!

Alice Through the Looking-Glass
continues in repertory until October 12.
The forecast for each performance is bright,
with a brief shower of jellybeans.

Leaving Stratford

Such sweet sorrow, as Shakespeare said.
Leaving Stratford is always hard but
we have learned to choose how we
feel and so we are not sad it's over,
we are happy it happened, or maybe
we feel something more sophisticated
like soldage as we leave Stratford
thinking about how great it was and I
add this trip to Stratford to all my
other trips to Stratford to see Shakespeare
starting in high school and continuing
through university and then every year as
a high school teacher plus two summers as
a teacher taking drama courses and other
summer trips including last summer like
this summer and I remember the summer
I studied English and Drama in England
and flew back to Canada in time to catch
a play at Stratford just days after seeing
Shakespeare at the National Theatre in
London and you cannot compare two
great theatrical traditions on just two plays
but I have to say, at the risk of offending
everyone in England, that Canada's
Shakespeare was far superior, and now
that I've spent a year in China and have
a new perspective on Canada as well as
tourism and development and culture
I look at Stratford with new eye and
envision it developed even more so it's
an even greater attraction with a
beach nearby and a casino and twice
as many theatres and more Canadian
content and even more Shakespeare and
more big American musicals and maybe
no definitely a French theatre and an
Italian opera hall and a concert hall by
the casino and great places for theatre
from China, Japan, and everywhere.

And an airport and a high speed train.
And I can hardly wait to come back
to Stratford again.

Toronto Poetry

A lot of poetry has been written about Toronto
and at least one song has been written about
the highway called The 401, but writing poetry
about the highways around Toronto is
something that just isn't done. We write
Southern Ontario Gothic, about people with
profound problems, not highways or super
highways linking Toronto to Stratford or
Toronto to Hamilton, Niagara On The Lake,
Niagara Falls, London, Detroit, Western
Ontario, South Western Ontario, Paris,
Ontario, this green landscape of rolling
flatlands with the Niagara Escarpment in
and Rattlesnake Point in the centre of it
with Highway 401 cutting through it, a
black ribbon in the forest with fields of
corn and four lanes of bumper-to-bumper
traffic, all new cars, the latest models,
the top end, no longer just from the Big
Four auto-makers, but still some cars from
Detroit and Oakville, and more from
South Korea and Japan, and so many people
streaming in to Toronto from Stratford,
London, Hamilton, so you guess there must be
something special happening in the big city
on the weekend as usually the traffic is
heavy going the other way as the millions
of people who live in the city head out of
town on Friday night but this Friday night
millions of people were going to Toronto
to see the Blue Jays play a double-header
on the weekend, to see the big Indy car
race in Toronto, to see a Katy Perry concert,
and there was a Salsa Festival on St. Clair
Avenue, four big special events on top of
the city's many regular attractions, so
there we were, stopped on the 401, several
times, travelling at low speeds, speeding up
for short stretches, stopping, starting, seeing

the same cars again and again, watching
one jet after another fly overhead, flying
out of Pearson International, heading west
to Detroit, Chicago, Winnipeg, Vancouver,
Los Angeles, Australia, Japan, South Korea,
maybe even China, and in from the east,
bringing in more people from New York City
for the big weekend in Toronto and we
realized our usual route past Yorkdale
down the Allen Expressway to Eglinton
would be so crammed with cars it would
add another hour to a trip that was taking
twice as long as usual so we tried going
down Avenue Road and it appeared to be
clear so it felt as though we were witnessing
a miracle as we zipped down from the
jam-packed highway to The Eglinton Way
in seconds, maybe a few minutes, after
hours on The 401 but being forced to
go slow on a super-highway after a week in
Stratford to see the Shakespeare Festival
plus other plays is not such a bad thing as
you can see it as a metaphor about
what to do with the rest of your life or
a preview of life in Canada and in the
West and all over the world in the near
future, perhaps, or you can just be
happy that everybody had to slow down and
play it safe instead of flying down the
highway at 120 and noticing nothing about
the landscape of green fields and forest
with jet airplanes in the blue skies and
nobody shooting them down, unlike
what was happening in Russia or the
area Russia is fighting over, called Ukraine,
and the air is clear here, unlike China,
with its late industrial revolution fuelled by
coal, taking so many manufacturing jobs
out of southern Ontario and the U.S.A. as
everything is now made in China and now
China is looking for English teachers like

me as so many people there want to leave
that big crowded country for North America
to see our wilderness and experience the
freedom of democracy, which gave us
Rob Ford as the mayor of Toronto and
Stephen Harper as the prime minister of
Canada, or maybe they just want to
get rich doing business in the land of
capitalism and materialism and create
links between Asia and North America
and after a week in Stratford after
a year in China I am thinking it would be
a great business idea to copy Stratford and
re-create it in China as China has replicated
other places in the West so the Chinese
people don't have to travel to Paris or
England and Stratford, China, would be
a popular attraction anywhere in the big
country of 1.4 billion but especially in a
place like Dalian, where I live, as there is
no place like Dalian, with the Black
Mountains beside the Yellow Sea, the best
air in Asia, a short flight from Beijing,
Shanghei, Hong Kong, Tokyo, and Seol,
South Korea, if not North Korea, and
the part of the old Soviet Union we
knew as Siberia and as I drive the
Kia I rented from Stratford to Toronto
I'm relatively not unhappy about how
the history of the world has turned out
after the War in Korea, the Second
World War, the Cold War, the history of
China over the past century and the last
five thousand years, not to mention the
short history of Canada and the rich
history of the Western world which
has given us great literature celebrated
beautifully in Stratford, in southern
Ontario, halfway between Alice
Munro's hometown and the city where
Margaret Atwood lives, just south of

my old hometown which was the
birthplace of Norman Bethune and
1.4 billion Chinese people would love to
visit this place and some would like to
live here so it would be a great idea to
copy Stratford and also some other
parts of southern and central Ontario
as a Canadian and Western culture
theme park with more than four
theatres celebrating Shakespeare and
the literature of the world outside
China plus the literature and culture
of China and we could call it
Toronto, China, or Stratford, China,
or Southern Ontario, China, or,
for marketing purposes, Western
World, China. Now there's a concept
that would take millions to develop
or maybe billions but it would make
billions year after year for many years
to come as China develops fast with
its industrial revolution turning into a
consumer revolution that will change it
into a futuristic wonderland where
East meets West and combines the best
of both with what we have learned over
the past century and the last millennium
and the five thousand years of history
on this planet that we have treated like a
garbage dump but still looks so beautiful
in many places, especially Canada from
coast to coast to coast, as I noticed when
I flew over it, on Canada Day, and the
section called Southern Ontario, which
I drove through, slowly, in July of 2014
on my way from Stratford to Toronto
one summer in Canada on holiday, home
from China for a couple of months and
what better way to spend my time than
a trip to Stratford for a week of plays and
writing and with my friend from the old

days when we were the stars of our
Grade One class at the North Ward Public
School in Gravenhurst, just starting to
learn and teach English at the start of
our lives which would be so full of
culture with her acting in movies in
New York City and going to L.A. for
Hollywood movies and me writing
hundreds of books and the two of us
coming together again decades later to
write about it all and celebrate the best of
Western civilization on a road trip from
Toronto to Stratford and home in the
summer of 2014 while we tried to
forget about global warming and the
other warnings about impending
global disasters and enjoy the best of
the West while formulating a plan to
take it to the Far East and make big
bucks replicating Stratford in China
and making it even more of a cultural
theme park celebrating the best of
the East and the West.

About the author ....

Canadian author Martin Avery, Hons. B.A., B.Ed., M.F.A., A.Q., Hons. Spec. Eng., D.I.S.H., now living in China, wrote 100 books set in the West and is now working on 100 books set in the East. After winning the Balzac Award for poetry, he was inspired to write 100 books, like Balzac, called The Human Comedy.

He was the Arts Department Head of the high school in Norman Bethune's hometown and is now English Department Head at Maple Leaf in Dalian, China. He's the founder of A Novel Marathon, the Muskoka Novel Marathon, The Great Canadian Winter Novel Marathon, the Toronto Novel Marathon, et cetera.

In addition to being an author and educator, he is a Reiki master, Zen meditation teacher, and qigong instructor.

He won the Most Prolific Poet Award at the Scugog Poetry Marathon and the Balzac Poetry Award.

The Great Wall Of China Books Series
1. From Bethune's Birthplace To The People's Republic Of China (memoir)
2. Swimming To China (poetry)
3. Mo Yan And Me (short novel)
4. Far Away, Dalian, Far Away (travel)
5. A Trip Around Lake Muskoka With Norman Bethune (short novel)
6. In Love And War
7. Chinese Kisses (poetry)
8. My Chinese Metamorphosis (poetry)
9. Hockey Night In China (non-fiction)
10. An Intro To Acupuncture And TCM (non-fiction)
11. Norman Bethune's Tears Cure Cancer (novel)
12. Bethune Returns To China (novel)
13. Bethune's Time (novel)
14. The Bethune Trilogy: A Trip Around Lake Muskoka With Norman Bethune, Bethune's Tears Cure Cancer, Bethune Returns To China
15. Good News From China (found poetry)
16. Suzanne Takes You Down (novel)
17. The Woman Who Was Picked Up By A Monk (poetry)
18. Bethune Buttons (poetry)
19. Dear China: Love Letter Poems
20. Dalian: A Long Poem (poetry)
21. The Way Of The Dragon (novel)
22. Past And Future Lives In China (fiction)
23. Love And Death In China (duology)
24. The Beijing-Vancouver Express: Connecting Toronto To Dalian, China to Canada
25. Dalian: A Long Poem
26. Toronto: A Long Poem
27. Toronto And Dalian: Two Long Poems
28. The Timeless Universal Etheric Library (poetry)
29. Oh Canada: A Long Poem On Canada Day
30. Holocaust Healing (novel)
31. My Chinese Enchantment (poetry)
32. Gravenhurst And China: A Long Poem
33. Crazy For Stratford: A Very Long Poem
34. A Midsummer Night's Dream In Stratford: A Very Long Poem
35. Stratford, China: A Long Poem

1. Poetry Night In Muskoka
2. How To Make Love In A Muskoka Chair
3. Al Purdy's Ghost
4. Twilight At The Museum
5. What Balzac Said
6. Identical Strangers
7. Zen Forest Haiku
8. Celebrating Global Warming
9. Ya Ya Yakupov!
10. Swimming To China
11. Chinese Kisses
12. My Chinese Metamorphosis
13. Good News From China
14. The Woman Who Was Picked Up By A Monk
15. Bethune Buttons
16. Dear China: Love Letter Poems
17. Dalian: A Long Poem
18. Toronto: A Very Long Poem
19. Toronto And Dalian: Two Very Long Poems
20. Oh Canada: A Long Poem On Canada Day
21. Canada From China: A Long Eulogy
22. My Chinese Enchantment
23. Gravenhurst And Bethune And China: A Long Poem
24. Crazy About Stratford: A Very Long Poem
25. A Midsummer Night's Dream In Stratford: A Very Long Poem
26. Stratford, China: A Long Poem

www.ingramcontent.com/pod-product-compliance
Lightning Source LLC
Chambersburg PA
CBHW031410040426
42444CB00005B/502